THIS PUBLICATION IS MADE POSSIBLE BY THE FOLLOWING:

FHC, INC.

HERMAN AND LaDONNA MEINDERS

THE SAMUEL ROBERTS NOBLE FOUNDATION

PHILLIPS PETROLEUM COMPANY

ARCHIE W. DUNHAM, CHAIRMAN, PRESIDENT AND CEO, CONOCO, INC.

RAYMOND JERDY AND ANNE GARY

LOVE'S COUNTRY STORES, INC.

OKLAHOMA NATURAL GAS COMPANY

THE House of Oklahoma Built

A HISTORY OF THE OKLAHOMA GOVERNOR'S MANSION

BY BETTY CROW AND BOB BURKE

FOREWORD BY CATHY KEATING

OKLAHOMA'S FIRST LADY

SERIES EDITOR, KENNY A. FRANKS

ASSOCIATE EDITOR, GINI MOORE CAMPBELL

ISBN 1-885596-16-2
Library of Congress Catalog Number 2001089958
Printed in Hong Kong by Colorprint Offset

Designed by Carol Haralson

OKLAHOMA HERITAGE ASSOCIATION
201 Northwest Fourteenth Street
Oklahoma City, Oklahoma 73103

OTHER BOOKS BY BOB BURKE

From Oklahoma To Eternity: The Life of Wiley Post and the Winnie Mae
Lyle Boren: Rebel Congressman
These Be Thine Arms Forever
3,500 Years of Burkes
The Stories and Speeches of Lyle H. Boren
Corn, Cattle, and Moonshine
Like a Prairie Fire
Push Back the Darkness
The Irish Connection
Lyle H. Boren: The Eloquent Congressman
Dewey F. Bartlett: The Bartlett Legacy
Glen D. Johnson, Sr.: The Road to Washington
An American Jurist: The Life of Alfred P. Murrah
Mike Monroney: Oklahoma Liberal
Roscoe Dunjee: Champion of Civil Rights
Out From the Shadows: The Life of John J. Harden
Abe Lemons: Court Magician
Glory Days of Summer: The History of Baseball in Oklahoma
Alice Robertson: Oklahoma Congresswoman
Victor Wickersham: Your Best Friend
Historic Oklahoma: An Illustrated History
Bryce Harlow: Mr. Integrity
Good Guys Wear White Hats: The Life of George Nigh

DEDICATED TO THE

FIRST FAMILIES WHO HAVED LIVED

IN THE GOVERNOR'S MANSION

Henry Simpson Johnston and Ethel Littleton Johnston, 1928-1929

William Judson Holloway and Amy Arnold Holloway, 1929-1931

William Henry "Alfalfa Bill" Murray and Mary Alice Hearrell Murray, 1931-1935

Ernest Whitworth Marland and Lydie Roberts Marland, 1935-1939

Leon Chase Phillips and Myrtle Ellenberger Phillips, 1939-1943

Robert Samuel Kerr and Grayce Breene Kerr, 1943-1947

Roy Joseph Turner and Jessica Grimm Turner, 1947-1951

Johnston Murray and Willie Emerson Murray, 1951-1955

Raymond Dancel Gary and Emma Mae Purser Gary, 1955-1959

James Howard Edmondson and Jeannette Bartleson Edmondson, 1959-1963

Henry Louis Bellmon and Shirley Osborn Bellmon, 1963-1967

Dewey Follett Bartlett and Ann Smith Bartlett, 1967-1971

David Hall and Jo Evans Hall, 1971-1975

David Lyle Boren and Janna Lou Little Boren, 1975

David Lyle Boren, 1976

David Lyle Boren and Molly Shi Boren, 1977-1979

George Patterson Nigh and Donna Skinner Nigh, 1979-1987

Henry Louis Bellmon and Shirley Osborn Bellmon, 1987-1991

David Lee Walters and Rhonda Smith Walters, 1991-1995

Francis Anthony Keating, II and Catherine Heller Keating, 1995-

Contents

Oh if these walls could talk! I still remember the first time I ever walked into Oklahoma's governor's mansion, an aging but still sturdy house that had been occupied by 16 other first families. As the seventeenth couple to inherit temporary custody of this grand old home, Frank and I had more questions than answers: How did our predecessors cope with the public attention? What is it like to have a president or a famous author drop by for lunch? For those who enjoyed good times, did the walls resound with laughter and joy? For those who faced impeachment or economic depression or war, were the nights long and lonely? Would there still be time for those family dinners and holiday celebrations we had always treasured?

The answers came in time, and yes the walls did talk. We learned the lore and some of the legends of the governor's mansion—from the tale that "Alfalfa Bill" Murray's ghost still resides here to the visible evidence of past restoration efforts undertaken by former first families.

Still, it was culture shock to walk in, unpack, and begin the business all state first families must face—becoming a center of attention, shedding the comfortable ordinariness of daily life, and donning new roles and new responsibilities. One of our first responsibilities was clear, to honor the heritage of this old and colorful home, because we knew it belonged to the people, and to history.

I asked for advice. Former First Lady Donna Nigh told of opening the entire mansion for public tours. Most nights she would come home and find notes poked under her pillow, asking her to "please talk to the governor" about this or that current issue on behalf of an anonymous constituent. "By all means host tours," Donna suggested, "but don't include the bedroom. Even first families need some privacy!"

Shirley Bellmon told of her efforts to instill a little healthy humility in her children during her husband's first term as governor back in the 1960s. "Don't go about bragging that your daddy is governor," she told the Bellmon daughters. One day a neighbor knocked on the kitchen door to borrow a cup of sugar. It was that kind of time, and the Bellmons are that kind of people. But when the neighbor asked young

First Lady Cathy Keating. Courtesy Jim Argo.

Gail if she was the governor's daughter, she politely replied, "That's not what my Mommy says."

Seventeen families. Seventy-plus years and counting. If these walls could talk!

Henry Johnston, so cruelly impeached; William Holloway, who once was a high school principal; the colorful and exotic "Alfalfa Bill" Murray, who plowed up the mansion grounds to plant crops for hungry Depression victims; Ernest W. Marland and the mysterious Lydie; the reliable and solid Leon Phillips; Robert S. Kerr, who left the mansion to become one of the century's most powerful United States Senators; Roy Turner, whose first love was always his ranch; Johnston Murray, who lived here as a boy and returned as governor, taking the oath from this father, "Alfalfa Bill"; Raymond Gary, one of the most honorable men who ever led our state; J. Howard Edmondson, fiery young revolutionary who died too soon; Henry Bellmon, first Republican and first to serve two non-consecutive full terms; Dewey Bartlett, a man of great virtue and vast courage; David Hall, whose personal failings betrayed a genial exterior; David Boren, the "boy wonder" who went on to become one of Oklahoma's great statesmen; George Nigh, first to serve two back-to-back terms; Henry Bellmon again, David Walters, and now—my husband, Frank Keating.

The First Ladies too: from Ethel Johnston to Shirley Bellmon, they all served as models, using their unofficial but highly visible positions to advance important causes, from war relief to helping Oklahomans harmed by disaster. And the children: there is a statue on the mansion grounds symbolizing the children. It is surrounded by bricks engraved with their names, a reminder that it is not easy to be young and under the spotlight of a parent's public and political successes and failures. There's even a small pet cemetery, resting place for cherished dogs and cats that never knew they lived in a governor's mansion, and were loved even more because they brought a happy, rowdy hominess to this place.

Oh, if these walls could talk!

Well, now they do. Thanks to Betty Crow and Bob Burke, you hold in your hands the first single-volume text and picture history of the Oklahoma governor's mansion. It is the product of much research. During our extensive restoration projects in 1995 and 1996, Frank and I and the many architects, decorators, and historical experts who helped bring the mansion back to life, researched the old photos and articles. Later, I was able to include details about the mansion in another book, *Our Governors' Mansions*, which visited all of America's "little White Houses." As restoration work was completed, Betty labored for more than two years to compile a comprehensive historical scrapbook about the mansion. Now the products of all those efforts have been brought together, with additional research, in a book whose last chapter is always to be written.

The mansion is still changing. Most recently, we formed Friends of the Mansion, Inc., a non-profit foundation to preserve this home into the new century. Phillips Petroleum, an Oklahoma company that once drilled oil wells on the mansion and Capitol grounds, helped construct the magnificent Phillips Pavilion, which vastly expanded the mansion's space for entertainment and large public functions. Tours are back on the schedule (We do rope off the bedroom—thank you, Donna!) and the mansion even has a small gift shop where visitors can acquire fine Oklahoma treasures. This book will be sold there, and like everything else in the shop, its sale will benefit Friends of the Mansion, Inc., along with the Oklahoma Heritage Association, which will also profit from proceeds to launch educational outreach programs about the mansion and those who have lived here.

Our restoration efforts sought to bring the mansion's past alive. So does this wonderful book. As you open the pages, you are stepping back through history, an intimate witness to events that spanned most of the century and that helped shape the character of our state.

Listen to the walls!

CATHY KEATING
First Lady of Oklahoma

We are indebted to many people who made the publication of this book possible. First Lady Cathy Keating and her staff, including Christy Alcox, Director of Special Projects, and Barbara Jobe, Chief of Staff to the first lady, were wonderful partners in the research, writing, and final review of the photographs and text. Splendid editorial assistance came from Barbara Brinkman.

We were fortunate to receive first hand knowledge of living in the governor's mansion from members of former first families. They include Robin Johnston; Gertrude Johnston Walton; Helen and Judge William J. Holloway, Jr.; Lois Ann Phillips Berndt; Martha Wallace Phillips; Lou and Robert S. Kerr, Jr.; Kay Kerr Adair; Anne and Gerdy Gary; Mona Mae Gary Waymire; Jeanne Edmondson; Patty Edmondson Zimmer; Nancy Hall Zumwalt; William H. Murray, III; Patricia Bellmon Copeland; Gail Bellmon Wynne; Ann Bellmon McFerron; Joanie Bartlett Atkinson; Dewey F. Bartlett, Jr.; Michael Bartlett; Georgeann Nigh Duty; and Mike Mashburn.

Special thanks to former First Ladies Ann Bartlett Burke, Donna Nigh, Molly Boren, the late Shirley Bellmon, Jo Hall, and Rhonda Walters and Governor Frank Keating and former Governors George Nigh, David Boren, Henry Bellmon, David Hall, and David Walters.

The following is an exhaustive list of the wonderful Oklahomans who assisted in the project: Betty Freeman; Mandy Howard; Barbara Smith; Margaret Worrell; Eric Dabney; Betty Price, Director, Oklahoma Arts Council; Georgiana Rymer; Chester Cowen; Bill Welge; Judith Michener; Jeff Briley; Rodger Harris; Bill Moore; Mary Ann Blochowiak; Scott Dowell; and Delbert Amen at the Oklahoma Historical Society; Annette Ryan, University of Central Oklahoma Archives; Fred Marvel, Oklahoma Tourism and Recreation Department; Bonnie Crawford, Okemah Public Library; John Lovett, University of Oklahoma Western History Collection; Ethel Smyth; and Imogene Johnson.

Others are LaDonna Brown, Chickasaw Council House Museum; Kay Bond, Cherokee Strip Museum; the late Opal Hartsell Brown;

Kathy Adams, Marland Mansion; Carol Spindle, Robert S. Kerr Museum; Kirk Rodden, Murray State College; Tammi Willis, Oklahoma Christian University; LuCelia Wise; Terry Griffith, Harn Homestead; Jim Argo; Stuart Ostler, State Capitol photographer; Shane Culpepper; Michael Ives; Ackerman McQueen Advertising; Mrs. M. J. Vanderventer; Kelly Crow, *Oklahoma Today* Magazine; and Molly Fleming, *Tulsa People* Magazine.

Others are Kathy Jackel, Oklahoma Secretary of State's office; Peggy Wilhoit, Legislative Services; Melvina Heisch, deputy state Historic Preservation Officer; Al Radfar, Ace Bookbinding Company; Mr. and Mrs. Carl Bills; Jimi Sagers, Paper Tree; Merrill Ahrens, Custom Graphics; Mary Dellafield; Amy Lucas; Jeanette Glasgow, Creative Memories consultant; Herschal Crow, Lee Office Equipment; Sally Ferrell; Kay Revell; Mary Duffe; State Senator Gilmer Capps; and State Representative David Braddock.

Carol Campbell, Melissa Hayer, Mary Phillips, Robin Davison, Billie Harry, and Linda Lynn at the Oklahoma Publishing Company archives opened their file cabinets full of historic photographs of the mansion and its occupants. Kitty Pittman, Mary Hardin, Adrienne Butler, Melecia Caruthers, Marilyn Miller, Vicki Sullivan, and Tom Crimm at the Oklahoma Department of Libraries were invaluable.

Thanks also to the staffs at the Tulsa County Library, Altus Public Library, Jan Eric Cartwright Law Library, and the Carl Albert Center at the University of Oklahoma.

A special tribute is accorded the Oklahoma Heritage Association, its chairman of the board Lee Allan Smith, president Dr. Paul Lambert, and incredible editors Dr. Kenny Franks and Gini Moore Campbell.

Thanks to the following brave souls who reviewed the early manuscripts of the book: Molly Boren, Donna Nigh, Shirley Bellmon, Jo Hall, Rhonda Walters, Connie Irby, Ruth Moore, Sue Laster Davidson, Chimene Burke, Sheila Parr, Betty Price, Louise Painter, Glenda Carlile, Sally Ferrell, and Dina Deupree.

Finally, thanks to our spouses, Herschal Crow and Chimene Burke, who were patient and understanding as we spent countless hours working and reworking the manuscript to its final form.

BOB BURKE
BETTY CROW

OKLAHOMA WAS MORE THAN TWO DECADES OLD
BEFORE IT PROVIDED AN OFFICIAL RESIDENCE
FOR ITS GOVERNOR AND HIS FAMILY. UNTIL 1928
OKLAHOMA'S CHIEF EXECUTIVES LIVED IN
PRIVATE HOMES AND HOTELS.

FINALLY A HOME FOR THE FIRST FAMILY

AFTER STATEHOOD in 1907, the first governor, Charles N. Haskell, busied himself with the affairs of establishing a new state, carved from Oklahoma and Indian territories. A statewide election was held June 11, 1910, to change the location of the state capital from Guthrie to Oklahoma City. Later that year, in December, 1910, during Haskell's last month as governor, House Bill 3 authorized the governor to accept donated land on Northeast 23rd Street in Oklahoma City for a State Capitol and an Executive Mansion.

A 1913 architect's conception of an executive mansion for Oklahoma's governor and his family was far different from the mansion built in 1928. Courtesy Oklahoma Historical Society.

Early Oklahoma leaders suggested building a governor's mansion on the ridge southeast of the State Capitol. This is a *Daily Oklahoman* artist's conception of what the mansion would look like from the south steps of the Capitol. It was later decided that the land southeast of the Capitol should be reserved for larger state buildings. It is now the site of the Wiley Post Building. Courtesy Oklahoma Publishing Company.

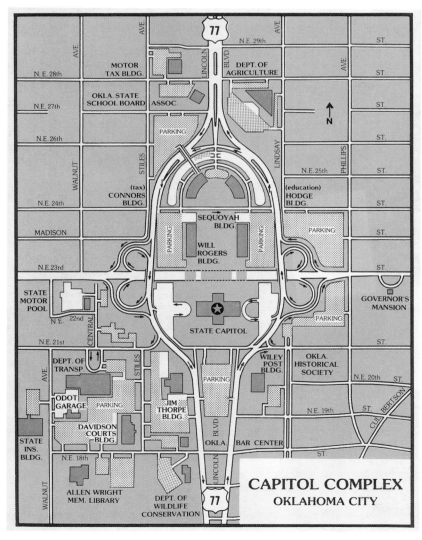

CAPITOL COMPLEX
OKLAHOMA CITY

Above: During construction of the governor's mansion in 1928, owners of nearby property planned to build a two-story office and apartment building. The proposed building, illustrated in the photograph above, would have been virtually on the doorstep of the mansion. After a lengthy court battle, the City of Oklahoma City's decision to deny a building permit to the property owners was upheld. The decision was part of a plan to build state buildings in an orderly manner around the State Capitol. Courtesy Oklahoma Publishing Company.

Left: The governor's mansion, far right, in relation to the State Capitol and other state office buildings in 2001. The state office complex grew as the size of government expanded. Courtesy Oklahoma Department of Central Services.

Lee Cruce, who followed Haskell as chief executive in 1911, promoted the construction of a State Capitol and designated a plot of land two blocks east of the present State Capitol as the site of an official governor's residence. An Oklahoma City architectural firm, Layton, Wemyss, Smith, and Hank, drafted plans for an elaborate mansion. However, Cruce's troubled administration and subsequent efforts by Governor Robert L. Williams to complete the State Capitol overshadowed attempts in the legislature to set aside sufficient money to build a permanent home for the governor and his family. The designated site for a governor's residence would remain a prairie for another 16 years.

By the 1920s, the site where most observers expected an official residence to be built was where the Wiley Post Building was constructed southeast of the State Capitol that sat boldly on a hill overlooking more than 100 acres owned by the state. That was the site for a mansion suggested by George Kessler who had planned the layout for state buildings that might someday surround the Capitol.

As state finances improved from tax collections on the vast production in Oklahoma's oil-boom fields, talk of appropriating money for a governor's residence was revived in 1926, during the final year of the administration of Governor Martin E. Trapp.

Henry S. Johnston was sworn in as Oklahoma's seventh governor in January, 1927. Within weeks, the state legislature, in House Bill 35, authorized the Board of Public Affairs to spend $75,000 for a governor's mansion and garage and an additional $25,000 on furnishings, landscaping, grading, and paving.

Some proponents of building an official residence for the governor scoffed at the appropriation, suggesting that a governor's home costing only $75,000 should never be called a "mansion." Bob Gilliam, secretary of the Board of Public Affairs, told a newspaper reporter, "Some day Oklahoma will have a $500,000 governor's mansion. Henry Johnston doesn't care about a huge mansion. He is content with a home and place where he can live respectably and entertain that way. Perhaps a governor of more wealth, who would stage big parties, would want a larger mansion."

With only $75,000 set aside for construction of the governor's mansion, its design presented a giant problem for the architectural firm selected to develop plans for the structure. Drawings by Layton, Hicks and Forsyth of Oklahoma City suggested a $200,000 mansion, a two-story home with two wings to be built of limestone. The *Oklahoma City Times* said "the smell of politics" entered the construction project at

The mansion during construction in the summer of 1928. The small garage, built of leftover boards, is seen at left. The garage was dwarfed by the three-story limestone mansion. Newspapers criticized the state for building a $75,000 governor's mansion and adding a $200 garage. Actually, the leftover boards and materials for the garage cost only $80. The garage was replaced the following year because of the embarrassment over the shoddy construction. Courtesy Oklahoma Publishing Company.

that point. Because he was about to be impeached and removed from office, Governor Johnston's enemies wanted the project halted "until the status of the administration is more clearly defined."

Amid speculation that $75,000 might only be sufficient to build a governor's residence that might later need to be enlarged, Johnston threatened to call the legislature into special session. The Board of Public Affairs was torn by the questions, "Shall we start a mansion? Or shall we build a home?" The board weighed its options. One member suggested using the $75,000 appropriation to build a single wing of the proposed large mansion. Another cooler head warned of "cluttering up the capitol grounds with a building wholly incompatible with the architecture of the capitol building and one which would be an eyesore for the future generations to gaze upon."

Contractors bidding on the construction of the executive mansion cut their bids to $98,000 by October, 1927. However, the Board of Public Affairs was determined to build a mansion in keeping with the architectural design of the State Capitol and within the $75,000 allocated by the legislature for the home.

Governor Johnston and his family lived in an apartment house on Northwest 17th Street while the Board of Public Affairs struggled in the fall of 1927 to reach a consensus on what kind of official residence to build. Hopes of convincing the legislature to appropriate $200,000 for a governor's residence vanished, prompting the board to instruct the architects to scrap plans for building only a single wing of the mansion. Instead Layton, Hicks and Forsythe were ordered to prepare a plan for a finished building at a cost of $75,000.

By November, 1927, realizing that a small mansion would look out of place on the high terrace southeast of the State Capitol, the Board of Public Affairs, with the support of Governor Johnston, decided to build the new executive mansion on the narrow strip of state-owned land east of the Capitol, in the middle of a five-acre tract, even though streetcar tracks had to be moved to give contractors access to the building site.

The governor's mansion as viewed from the east steps of the State Capitol. The mansion faced the Capitol rather than Northeast 23rd Street to the north. Courtesy Oklahoma Historical Society.

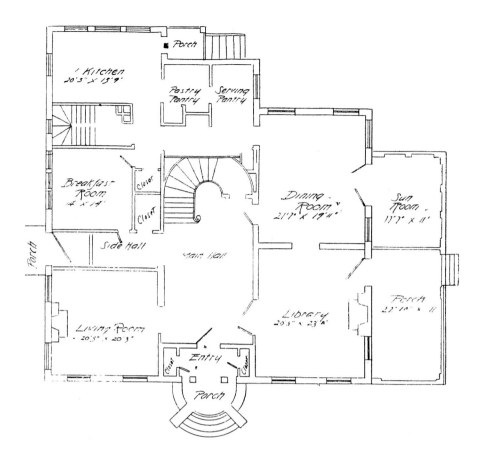

The architect's drawing of the proposed governor's mansion was approved in 1928 by the State Board of Public Affairs. The 19-room official residence was a scaled-down version of a mansion that originally was planned to.cost $200,000. Courtesy Oklahoma Publishing Company.

FIRST FLOOR

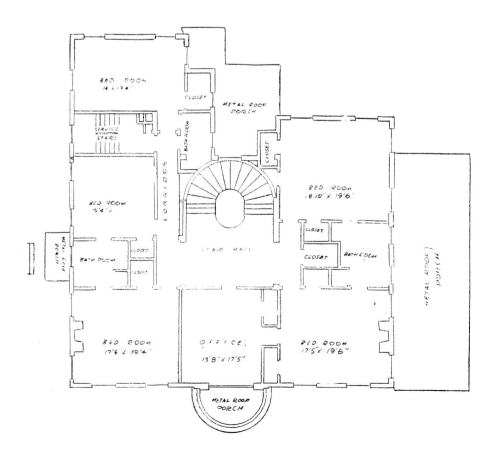

SECOND FLOOR

The revised plans allowed construction of a 19-room mansion. The first floor would contain a living room or music room, dining room, sunroom, library, breakfast room, and kitchen. Five bedrooms, a sleeping porch, three baths, and an office or sitting room would be on the second floor.

On the third floor would be a ballroom, 23 feet wide and 54 feet long, and three storage rooms. An elaborate staircase would connect the two floors from a large reception hall on the first floor. The basement would house a laundry, furnace, boiler, and fuel rooms.

Oklahomans were excited as the Board of Public Affairs solicited bids for the mansion. However, when 11 bids were received in January, 1928, the lowest, $87,130, was more than $10,000 above the $75,000 appropriated by the legislature. The low bidder, Smiser Construction Company of Oklahoma City, looked for ways to cut costs, including the idea of building the mansion of white brick, rather than limestone.

Negotiations between Smiser Construction and the Board of Public Affairs resulted in a return to the original plan of building the mansion of Indiana limestone, to conform with the construction of the State Capitol. It was decided to face the mansion west toward the Capitol, toward Phillips Avenue, rather than Northeast 23rd Street. Ground was broken and construction began in March of 1928.

Long before the exterior of the mansion was completed, First Lady Ethel Johnston began the laborious process of selecting plumbing fixtures, even though her husband's political troubles with the legislature must have caused her to wonder if she would ever live in the mansion.

Dozens of merchants insisted she see their best offerings before purchases were made. Money was tight making necessary the selection of plain, all-white bathroom and kitchen fixtures.

Smiser Construction ran out of money and materials from the $75,000 appropriation by the time construction began on a garage adjacent to the mansion. Using leftover building materials, the double-car garage, looking like a box next to the limestone mansion, cost less than $200. A spokesman for the Board of Public Affairs promised the garage was only "a temporary measure."

Not everyone was proud of the new mansion. Some said the building looked like a barn. Others criticized the governor and first lady for preparing to move into a house surrounded by barren land. Unperturbed, the first lady believed that trees could be planted around the mansion and that criticism of the landscaping would be forgotten in two or three years.

The mansion had one hot water tank and was heated by steam piped through iron radiators. There was no bathroom downstairs. The $300 per month operating budget hardly covered bills for electricity, water, and gas.

Newspapers followed with interest the first lady's furnishing of the mansion. Mrs. Johnston said, "After all, it is called a mansion, but it is not a mansion, only a large, comfortable home, built for durability and practicability more than anything."

With the help of interior decorators from Harbour Longmire Furniture Company in Oklahoma City, the first lady chose what she described as "plain, functional" furniture. She bought 167 light bulbs for $36.11; a Hoover sweeper for $78.75; 12 ice cream bowls for $11.25; a carpet sweeper for $7.90; drapes and rugs for $50.00; and a waffle iron and other kitchen equipment for $20.91. To complete purchases for furnishing the mansion, the first lady dipped into the $300 per month mansion maintenance account appropriated by the legislature.

The executive mansion was completed in early October, 1928, ready for the first family to move in.

Builders completed construction on the Oklahoma governor's mansion in early October, 1928, within the $75,000 budget approved by the state legislature. However, with little money left for landscaping, the mansion grounds remained bare. Courtesy Oklahoma Publishing Company.

Henry S. Johnston conducted an active law practice in Perry after he was ousted from office in 1929. Many Oklahomans believed he had been a victim of political persecution. He was respected by Oklahoma's leaders for decades. Courtesy Oklahoma Historical Society.

Governor Henry S. Johnston and First Lady Ethel Johnston led the grand march around the State Capitol to begin the January, 1927, inauguration. Courtesy Oklahoma Publishing Company.

GOVERNOR HENRY SIMPSON JOHNSTON AND HIS FAMILY SPENT THEIR FIRST NIGHT IN THE NEWLY COMPLETED OKLAHOMA GOVERNOR'S MANSION OCTOBER 11, 1928. IT WAS A QUIET NIGHT FOR THE GOVERNOR BECAUSE THE TELEPHONE IN THE MANSION HAD NOT YET BEEN INSTALLED. MAROONED IN THE MIDDLE OF A VAST EXPANSE OF UNLANDSCAPED PROPERTY, GOVERNOR JOHNSTON SAID HE RESTED BETTER THAN USUAL, ALTHOUGH HE MISSED THE JANGLE OF THE TELEPHONE.

IMPEACHMENT LOOMS

JOHNSTON, born in Indiana, December 30, 1870, settled in Perry, Oklahoma, in 1893, taking advantage of the opening of the Cherokee Outlet. He was a politician by nature and was elected to the Oklahoma Territorial Council in 1896. Johnston presided over the organizational phase of the Oklahoma Constitutional Convention.

He is credited with writing the state constitution's provisions on initiative and referendum. After Oklahoma joined the Union, Johnston served as President Pro Tempore of the first State Senate in Guthrie, where he met and married legislative reporter Ethel Littleton. Ethel was born in Kansas but spent most of her early years in Perry. Johnston twice ran unsuccessfully for Congress. He overcame charges that he supported the Ku Klux Klan and won the governor's race in 1926. Johnston was the first governor to open his inauguration with a prayer when he took office in January, 1927. About 20,000 people attended the inauguration on the south steps of the State Capitol. Governor Johnston's inauguration also was the first to be broadcast on radio and over loud speakers to the festive crowd.

The Johnstons held a grand inaugural ball at the Capitol. A newspaper account painted a vivid picture of activity on all floors, including "a variety of dancing, including moderns, old fashioned kinds, and the in-betweens." The ball was coordinated by Oklahoma City Chamber of Commerce manager Ed Overholser.

The ball began with a grand march of men and their ladies, decked out in velvet, chiffon, and lace gowns. The new first lady was the center of attention in her Parisian sequin dress of brown crepe, "fashioned with a long waist and flare skirt." A reporter commented, "With a gracious and kind word for all who passed her way, she captured the heart of the crowd."

Left: First Lady Ethel Johnston in her Paris-designed inaugural gown in January, 1927. The dress was golden brown crepe with trimmings of beads and sequins. She wore gold slippers with gold accessories to complete the costume. Courtesy Oklahoma Historical Society.

Above: The first family at the mansion door. Below: The first family at Christmas, 1928. Left to right, Gertrude, Robin, Governor Henry Johnston, Reba, First Lady Ethel Johnston, and Nell. The Johnstons lived in the mansion only a few months before Governor Johnston was impeached and removed from office by the state legislature. Courtesy Oklahoma Historical Society.

Above: First Lady Ethel Johnston and her four children shortly after moving into the governor's mansion in 1928. Left to right, Gertrude, Robin, the first lady, Reba, and Nell. The Johnston children were excited to learn that the big tops of the Barnum-Bailey Circus were set up across the street from the mansion. The circus and mansion were pictured together under a caption, "Three Rings and a Sideshow," an obvious reference to the small amount of money spent on the official residence of Oklahoma's governor and his family. Mrs. Johnston went about her task of furnishing the mansion, even though a cloud of pending impeachment hung over her husband during their occupancy of the mansion. Courtesy Oklahoma Publishing Company.

Swashbuckling national guard officers herded 15,000 visitors into the tightly-packed halls and rotundas of the Capitol. Many attendees never got close enough to the action to hear the music of the night.

Governor Johnston pushed through the legislature bills to increase state education spending and create a crippled children's hospital. He then fell out of grace with state legislators. The rift widened until the Oklahoma House of Representatives voted 11 articles of impeachment against Johnston in January, 1929. The State Senate conducted the impeachment trial during February and March, 1929. The voluminous testimony surrounding charges of illegally hiring state employees and calling out the national guard to prevent the Senate from meeting ran more than 5,000 pages.

During the impeachment trial, the first lady stood by her man. In fact, she sat by her man, accompanying her husband to the Senate trial and sat quietly behind the governor as witnesses called him everything but civil. Finally, the Senate, no doubt politically motivated, found Johnston guilty of a single charge of general incompetentcy.

He was the second Oklahoma governor to be impeached and removed from office. He lived out his life in Perry, practicing law, and serving one term in the Oklahoma State Senate. He died January 7, 1965, at age 94, one day after a proposal to soften his impeachment was introduced in the House.

While serving as first lady, Ethel Johnston wisely spent her allocated $25,000 in furnishing the Oklahoma governor's mansion. Mrs. Johnston, an attractive, slender brunette known as a fashion style setter, had

The kitchen in the new mansion was a housewife's dream with tile walls and a rubber tile floor and every built-in any woman could wish for in 1928. Courtesy Cherokee Strip Museum.

Left: The breakfast room was warmed by a radiator under the window. A newspaper reporter said the room was "gay with Spanish fittings." Visitors to the mansion appreciated the Spanish design of the room. Courtesy Oklahoma Publishing Company.

Below: The music room had canvassed walls, hand decorated in an apricot and gold mixture called "cuivre." Neapolitan damask brocade draperies of gold and apricot, with dark parchment woodwork, completed the décor. Courtesy Oklahoma Publishing Company.

Left: The library was a quiet room with glassed-in walnut bookshelves from floor to ceiling. Gold satin draperies blended with the ornate rug. This room was also used by the Johnstons as a family living room. Courtesy Oklahoma Historical Society.

Below: The mansion's first dining room had a barrel-shaped china cabinet of mahogany inlaid with walnut paneling. It was decorated with two medallions hand painted in oil. The mahogany and walnut inlaid sideboard was decorated with hand-carved scrolling. Twelve chairs surrounded the table that was made of mahogany with a walnut top. Courtesy Cherokee Strip Museum.

The mansion's third floor ballroom was not completed when the Johnstons moved into the executive residence. Only two chairs and a radiator for heat adorned the large room that had ivory walls and apple green woodwork. Courtesy Oklahoma Publishing Company.

walnut glassed-in bookcases built in the library. She purchased an old-fashioned globe and overstuffed chairs for the room that became a comfortable place for the family to gather. On the mantle was a ship of state. The first lady had canvas installed as the wall-covering for the music room of which a newspaper reporter wrote, "Neapolitan damask brocade draperies of gold and apricot, dark antique parchment woodwork and a charming sofa and arm chair lacquered in the parchment shade and hand-decorated will lend a unique atmosphere to this room."

Mrs. Johnston found she could not personally sweep three floors of carpet, dust hundreds of square feet of walls and a thousand furniture niches, polish an acre of hardwood floors, poke coal into the furnace, and pile logs in the fireplace during the winter months. The legislature came to her rescue and provided funds for a yard man and a maid.

Governor Johnston's salary was only $4,500 annually. Therefore the state legislature approved expenses up to $300 per month for upkeep of the mansion, provided the first family submitted receipts. The expense included maintenance of the residence and bills for water, gas, telephone, and electric service. The cost of groceries was not reimbursed, even if the Johnstons entertained at state functions.

The first lady carefully planned the sleeping quarters for the four Johnston children. Four-year-old Robin slept on a foldaway bed in his mother's bedroom. Reba, age eight, shared a rose and blue bedroom with eleven-year-old Gertrude. The eldest child of the first family, thirteen-year-old Nell, slept in a brightly painted green bedroom which

Governor Johnston's bedroom (immediately below) had a large four-poster bed, Byzantine damask copper-colored draperies, and walls canvassed and painted copper. The first lady's bedroom (photo at bottom) had a walnut suite and was decorated in apricot and green taffeta. Courtesy Oklahoma Publishing Company.

Facing page: Portraits of Governor Henry Johnston and First Lady Ethel Johnston were among items auctioned at an estate sale at their former Perry home in 1980. The portraits were only a small part of the heirlooms from a half-century of the Johnstons living in Perry. Courtesy Oklahoma Publishing Company.

First Lady Ethel Johnston was busy in civic affairs after she returned to Perry. She established the town's first Camp Fire Girls post. Here she is dressed in her Camp Fire Girls regalia. Courtesy Cherokee Strip Museum.

was connected by a green bathroom to the mansion guest room. The basement was turned into a gymnasium and children's playroom.

Sixty years after Robin Johnston lived in the mansion as a toddler, he recalled, "We were not only a close and happy family but enjoyed immensely the spaciousness and uniqueness that the home provided."

The Johnstons made their only Christmas in the mansion special. They were the first family to send an official Christmas card from the mansion to friends and family. Mrs. Johnston helped prepare a delicious Christmas dinner for a large gathering of relatives.

After Governor Johnston was impeached, the first lady went about the sad task of packing personal belongings and furniture to be moved to their new home, the upper apartments in a new building at 818½ East Drive in Oklahoma City. The Johnstons had lived in the governor's mansion less than seven months.

The first lady and Governor Johnston picked through china and kitchen gadgets, deciding which were theirs and which remained with the mansion. National guardsmen filled their trucks with the Johnston's belongings. The governor carried heavy boxes of books to the waiting trucks. The ten-foot-tall grandfather clock, a gift to the Johnston family from state employees, was transported by a separate truck to Johnston's private law office in Perry.

The Johnston children actually looked forward to having a yard in which to play. The bare clay around the mansion was not conducive to youngsters frolicking their hours away after school.

A few days after moving from the governor's mansion, the Johnstons returned home to Perry where more than 1,000 admirers greeted them. A band blared patriotic music as the Johnston touring car pulled in front of the courthouse. It was the same band that had sent the Johnstons off to Oklahoma City with a rousing victory march after the 1926 election.

After a long life of public service, Mrs. Johnston died in Perry December 27, 1977. She was grand secretary of the Order of Eastern Star in Oklahoma for 25 years. She enjoyed her membership in artist groups, often entering her paintings in competitions, and was a charter member and first president of the Cherokee Strip Historical Society. She also was the first chairman of the Noble County Red Cross Chapter and established Perry's first Camp Fire Girls post.

For more information on the Henry Johnston family, see:

Stewart, Roy P. with Pendleton Woods. *Born Grown* (Oklahoma City: Fidelity Bank, 1974)

Blackburn, Bob L. *Heart of the Promised Land, Oklahoma County* (Woodland Hills, California: Windsor Publications, Inc., 1982)

Fischer, LeRoy H., editor, *Oklahoma's Governors, 1907-1929: Turbulent Politics* (Oklahoma City: Oklahoma Historical Society, 1981)

AMY HOLLOWAY, THE WIFE OF LIEUTENANT GOVERNOR WILLIAM JUDSON HOLLOWAY, HAD NEVER BEEN INSIDE THE GOVERNOR'S MANSION WHEN THE TITLE OF FIRST LADY WAS THRUST UPON HER THE DAY GOVERNOR JOHNSTON WAS REMOVED FROM OFFICE, MARCH 20, 1929.

A NEW GOVERNOR ∞ AND A NEW GARAGE

THE HOLLOWAYS were at home when they received news by a runner from the Capitol that Johnston had been convicted. Holloway rushed to the Capitol and was sworn in as governor by Chief Justice Charles Mason of the Oklahoma Supreme Court.

Holloway was born December 15, 1888, in Arkadelphia, Arkansas, the son and grandson of Baptist preachers. He graduated from Ouachita College in Arkansas and the Cumberland University Law School in Tennessee. He served in the Oklahoma State Senate before he was elected Lieutenant Governor in 1926. As governor he reorganized the state highway department and pushed increased funding for higher education facilities. Holloway presided over a difficult transition in Oklahoma government between the boisterous and booming 1920s and the 1930s, dominated by Depression.

The new first lady was a devoted mother of her five-year-old son "Billy," the nickname for the enthusiastic William J. Holloway, Jr., who grew up to be a distinguished lawyer and longtime member of the United States Court of Appeals for the Tenth Circuit.

As Governor, William J. Holloway reorganized many agencies in state government to provide greater efficiency of operation. His reorganization of the State Highway Department brought more hard-surfaced roads to Oklahoma than had been built in any previous comparable period of time. Courtesy Oklahoma Historical Society.

Left: First Lady Amy Holloway and son Bill. Mrs. Holloway devoted her time to her family, church work, sewing, and reading. She made no secret that her priority as first lady was to make a good home for her husband and son. Courtesy Oklahoma Publishing Company.

Amy Arnold Holloway was born in Paducah, Kentucky, grew up in Texarkana, Arkansas, and graduated from Ouachita Baptist College in Arkadelphia, Arkansas. She met her future husband while teaching school in Hugo, Oklahoma, where he had set up a law practice after resigning as principal of Hugo High School. The two spotted each other across the room at a church social in 1915 and were married two years later.

The new first lady sparkled when she talked about her priority, making a comfortable and loving home for her husband and son. She was quick to tell about Billy's love for airplanes and stories about them. He would sit for hours listening to airplane stories. Mrs. Holloway said she had no political agenda and would stay in the background, pledging, "I will meet all social obligations of my husband's position as gracefully as possible."

The first lady received reporters as she packed china and clothing for the move from the Holloway home at 905 East 17th Street to the mansion. A reporter observed, "She wore a black felt beret pulled down over her glistening, bobbed, black hair and sparkling black eyes. She sank into a large armchair—A grate fire threw yellow shadows over her olive skin and rosy cheeks. She was a picture, and she didn't realize it."

Young Billy took over the first official news conference from his mother when he discovered that one of the reporters had actually been "up in a plane." Billy, "with his mother's brown eyes and a self-assured manner of entering a room," asked a hundred questions, "What made the plane fly? What made it turn around? Could a boy run a plane?" Billy always asked any visitor if they knew his hero, Charles Lindbergh, who had recently flown the Atlantic in his *Spirit of St. Louis*.

Top: As shrubs and bedding plants were added to the landscaping of the mansion grounds, the executive residence took on the appearance of a stately home. First Lady Amy Holloway hosted the first public open house at the governor's mansion in October, 1930. Oklahomans were excited about the opportunity to view the completed mansion and the landscaped grounds. Courtesy Oklahoma Historical Society.

The 1929 Oklahoma legislature appropriated $39,550 for improvements to the governor's mansion and grounds. An ornamental iron fence was installed along Northeast 23rd Street. Note the team of mules in the background that was used to hoist the iron into place. Courtesy Oklahoma Publishing Company.

A two-story garage was added east of the mansion and extensive landscaping was completed in late 1929 and early 1930. This photograph was taken April 11, 1930. Courtesy Oklahoma Historical Society.

An aerial view of the mansion in 1930 showed the formal rose garden given by the Oklahoma Federation of Women's Clubs. Note the boxwood hedges and arbor to the right of the gardens. Courtesy Oklahoma Publishing Company.

Left: Young Billy Holloway, right front, with playmates from the neighborhood surrounding the governor's mansion. Governor and Mrs. Holloway wanted a normal life for their son even though he lived in the mansion. They often invited neighborhood children to visit the executive residence. Courtesy Oklahoma Historical Society.

Right: William J. Holloway, Jr., on the west porch of the mansion in 1931. Holloway, like his father, became a lawyer and eventually served on the United States Court of Appeals for the Tenth Circuit. Courtesy William J. Holloway.

Above, left to right, First Lady Amy Holloway, Governor William J. Holloway, and William J. Holloway, Jr., at the World's Fair in Chicago, Illinois. Courtesy Oklahoma Historical Society.

The 1929 Oklahoma legislature recognized the need to build a decent garage for the governor's mansion. Senate Bill 91 provided an appropriation of $39,550 to construct a two-story garage, a fence around the mansion, landscaping, awnings for the windows, and additional furniture.

· The first lady began the enormous task of making the mansion a home. The threat of impeachment and the lack of funds had prevented the Johnstons from taking real interest in developing the expanse of land that surrounded the mansion. For more than a year the executive residence stood in the midst of bare dirt and weeds with a garage made of leftover boards.

After the fence was completed along Northeast 23rd Street, grass, flowers, and shrubs were added under the direction of landscape professionals from Oklahoma A & M College at Stillwater. A newspaper reflected, "Before the improvements, the governor's mansion was only a house; now it is a thing of beauty—one of the most beautiful homes in Oklahoma."

Landscape architect Don V. Shuhart and his helper, John Brown, built formal walks and a lily pool and planted a formal rose garden, innumerable shrubs, and weeping willows. Twenty silver cedar trees were transplanted to the mansion grounds from the lawn of the Payne County Courthouse in Stillwater.

Shuhart also cleared a wooded area and planted a vast lawn, in keeping with the colonial architecture of the mansion. The Oklahoma

Tenth Circuit Court of Appeals Judge William J. Holloway, Jr., left, and United States District Judge Ralph G. Thompson admire Judge Holloway's portrait unveiled at the federal courthouse in Oklahoma City in 1991. Courtesy Oklahoma Publishing Company.

Federation of Women's Clubs donated rose bushes to grace the nine rose beds south of the garage, one for each of the organization's nine districts in the state.

The first lady took an active part in planting the flowers and shrubs. She could often be seen in her work clothes helping workmen lower a rose bush into a freshly dug hole.

Mrs. Holloway was accustomed to cleaning her own home and cooking for her family. However, with new duties as first lady, she readily accepted the help of a maid and a cook.

Billy Holloway was especially excited about the new lily pond, which he called his fishpond. The large yard with soft grass gave him and his playmates a perfect spot to toss balls and tackle each other. Billy used the large ballroom on the third floor of the mansion as a playroom.

Judge Holloway wrote in 1998 about one occasion he recalled clearly. The *Graf Zeppelin*, the German lighter-than-air vehicle, flew over Oklahoma City one night. Excited, he and his family went out onto the small balcony and watched in the night sky, hoping for a view of the *Zeppelin*. Unfortunately, they never saw it, but the occasion was indelibly etched into his mind.

The Holloways hosted many family gatherings in their two years in the mansion. Parents, brothers, sisters, cousins, and second cousins came for large parties. On the Holloways' first Christmas Eve in the mansion, 18 family members spent the night. It was a joyous time.

Governor Holloway's last official act as governor of Oklahoma was special. He wrote his son a letter, the last instrument he signed as Oklahoma's chief executive. He told his son, "I sincerely hope that when you have grown to be a man that you and your mother can look back with pride upon the two years of my administration—My prayer and greatest ambition is that you may have good health and live to become a useful and upright citizen. To the accomplishment of this high purpose for you I shall devote my life."

Governor and Mrs. Holloway were respected Oklahoma leaders for the remainder of their lives. Holloway began a successful law practice after leaving the governor's mansion and never again ran for public office. He served under three different governors as the Oklahoma representative on the Interstate Oil Compact Commission. He died January 28, 1970.

First Lady Amy Holloway was a longtime member of Oklahoma City's St. Luke's Methodist Church where she served as president of the Women's Society of Christian Service. Mrs. Holloway also was president of the Wesley House Board and a member of the Bookmark Club and Blue Flower Garden Club. She died September 8, 1969.

For more information on the William J. Holloway family, see:

Fischer, LeRoy, editor. *Oklahoma's Governors, 1907-1929 Turbulent Politics* (Oklahoma
    City: Oklahoma Historical Society, 1981)

DURING THE GUBERNATORIAL CAMPAIGN OF
WILLIAM HENRY "ALFALFA BILL" MURRAY IN 1930,
THE FLAMBOYANT FORMER CHAIRMAN OF THE
OKLAHOMA CONSTITUTIONAL CONVENTION
PROMISED TO RENT THE GOVERNOR'S MANSION
TO GENERATE INCOME FOR THE STATE WHILE HE
AND HIS FAMILY LIVED IN THE MANSION'S
GARAGE.

William H. "Alfalfa Bill" Murray, left, and his aging father, U.D.T. Murray, at the younger Murray's inauguration January 12, 1931. Courtesy Oklahoma Historical Society.

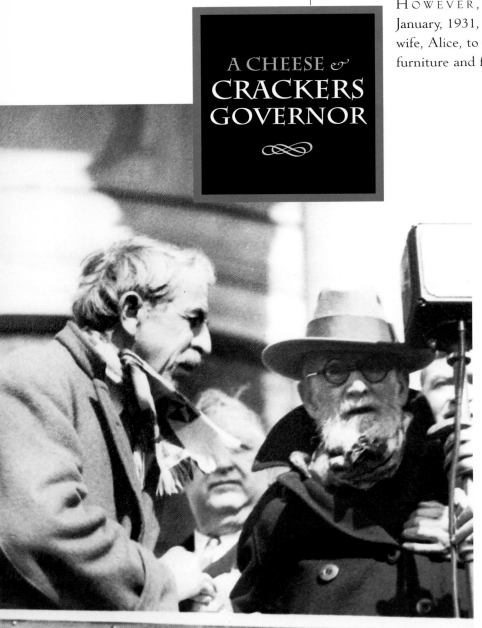

A CHEESE & CRACKERS GOVERNOR

HOWEVER, by the time Murray was inaugurated in January, 1931, he had changed his mind and dispatched his wife, Alice, to the mansion to determine what personal furniture and furnishings they should bring with them to their new home.

Murray, born November 21, 1869, in Collinsville, Texas, was a colorful character and one of the best-known politicians in Oklahoma's storied past. It is said that he received his nickname because of his expertise in growing alfalfa for livestock hay. He was a comeback gubernatorial candidate in 1930 after a long career as a cowpuncher, woodchopper, the first Speaker of the Oklahoma House of Representatives, United States Congressman from 1913-1917, farmer, teacher, and lawyer.

Mary Alice Hearrell Murray, born January 9, 1875, on the Blue River near Milburn, Oklahoma, was a Chickasaw princess, the niece of Chickasaw Governor Douglas Johnston. Known to her friends as "Gentle Alice," she acquired the graces of a fine lady, including learning fine needlework and the beaded art so treasured among her people. Her sense of humor and charm made her the pet of teachers and classmates at Bloomfield Academy for girls in what is now Bryan County, Oklahoma. Alice's Indian heritage was a romantic link between Indian Territory and the up and coming state that had so recently come of age.

The future first lady's courtship with Murray was primarily by mail. It was a

"Alfalfa Bill" Murray speaking at an organized labor rally at Soldier's Field in Chicago, Illinois, September 7, 1931. The "rough-at-the-edges" Oklahoma governor was an attractive presidential candidate for labor leaders and populists. At the 1932 Democratic National Convention former Oklahoma governor Henry S. Johnston nominated Murray for the Democratic presidential nomination, eventually won by Franklin D. Roosevelt. Courtesy Oklahoma Publishing Company.

The fashionable first lady in her v-necked inaugural dress of black lace. Mrs. Murray enjoyed "dressing up" and attending banquets and political rallies with her husband. Courtesy Oklahoma Publishing Company.

Victorian courtship of chaperoned visits and formal love letters. Late at night, after long days in court, the young lawyer Murray composed somewhat stilted but increasingly ardent letters to Mary Alice. Murray quoted from Robert Burns in a final appeal for Mary Alice's hand. They were married July 19, 1899, at Governor Johnston's home near Tishomingo.

Mrs. Murray, whose husband was serving in the United States House of Representatives, was called a "presiding angel over all lines of domestic endeavor." A newspaper reporter wrote, "There is one woman at least remaining in the world who can cook for a family of seven, do her sewing, bake her bread, launder the dainty little garments of her baby boy and her small daughter, yet find time to read." The future first lady of Oklahoma was described as "a comely young woman, well educated, devoted to books, to art, and to all that a refined and gentle nature craves."

First Lady Alice Murray hosted a unique quilting bee at the mansion. She invited one woman more than 70 years old from each of the state's 77 counties. Courtesy Oklahoma Publishing Company.

The governor's mansion was pictured on early Oklahoma postcards. Oklahomans were proud of their new executive mansion and were quick to use the postcards for correspondence to friends and family located throughout the nation. Courtesy Oklahoma Historical Society.

Governor's Mansion, Oklahoma City, Oklahoma   41C

PHOTO BY ROY CHRISTIAN   OKLAHOMA CITY

Mrs. Murray was a devoted mother and wife and believed a woman's life should revolve around her family. She advocated the idea that being a good wife and mother were the two most important privileges a woman could have. She was against women working outside the home, once saying, "Married women who are augmenting the family budget by working in stores and in offices could help their mates far better by attending to their household duties and economizing where possible. They might not be able to buy that new radio or car this year, but they would have the fun of saving for the purpose and watching the fund grow."

Mrs. Murray did not play bridge, calling it a waste of time. She believed bridge players should instead spend afternoons sewing for their own family or a poor child.

The future first lady was troubled by the influence of movies on families. Even though she and her children would occasionally attend a movie, she said, "So many of our young people, and elders too, have the cinema craze. Picture shows often put too many ideas into the heads of the impressionable." Mrs. Murray thought movies caused people to become dissatisfied with their lot in life and desire things not within their reach.

While her husband served in Congress, Mrs. Murray expanded the knowledge of her children by introducing them to the history of the nation's capital. She often packed a picnic lunch and set off on a junket to museums, galleries, and public buildings. Even with the splendor of Washington, D.C., Mrs. Murray missed her farm back in Oklahoma, especially the food from the farm. She said, "If only our farm was a little closer so we could use the plump hens, fine heifers and lambs, not to mention such vegetables as one never sees in Washington, and the honey, which is possible only where alfalfa grows."

Even though Governor Murray had been elected in 1930 in an austere "cheese and crackers" campaign, the Murray inaugural ball was anything but austere. After the new governor was sworn in by his 91-year-old father, Mrs. Murray hosted a gala event where the crowd was "so thick it was difficult for the dancers to maneuver." The first lady's inaugural dress of black lace was very much in fashion for the early 1930s. A touch of georgette and blonde lace outlined the deep V neckline. The skirt began at the normal waistline and "widened from the hips down to the floor."

The lush grass crop of "Alfalfa Bill" Murray on the mansion lawn sprang from his belief, based on a Biblical passage in Leviticus, that any homeowner should let the grass go to seed every seven years. The unsightly appearance of the mansion grounds was an embarrassment to neighbors and state officials. When the crop was harvested, it was sent to Murray State College at Tishomingo. Courtesy Oklahoma Publishing Company.

Oklahoma and the nation were in the midst of the Great Depression when Murray became governor. Thousands of Oklahomans were left homeless and jobless. The weather contributed to the problem in the Sooner State. A searing drought hit the southern plains and Oklahoma was wracked with dust storms and sand blew in such quantities that travelers lost their way, chickens went to roost at noon, airports closed, and trains stopped.

As Governor Murray began to tackle the formidable problems facing state government, the new first lady assumed her role as her husband's greatest promoter. She was well poised and gracious when she spoke of her companion of 32 years who was called the "Sage of Tishomingo."

The first event that Mrs. Murray hosted in the governor's mansion was an all-day quilting bee for ladies more than 70 years of age, one from each county in the state. The first lady saw her time in her new home as somewhat of a vacation. She had spent her first 32 years of married life raising children. Now she supervised maids to make her beds and clean the mansion. She had time in the afternoons to paint and listen to music. She was an ardent lover of music and drama.

A *Tulsa Daily World* reporter interviewed Mrs. Murray at the mansion in February, 1931, painting a poignant word picture, "The door was open wide. Streams of sunshine glinted down the stately entrance hall. From somewhere came sounds of radio music, a popular tune. From the region of the kitchen wafted a faint, yet unmistakable odor of boiling turnip greens, the governor's favorite vegetable."

The Murrays sent mixed signals to Oklahomans about their economic beliefs. Even though "Alfalfa Bill" Murray had even suggested renting out the governor's mansion, he and the first lady often rode about Oklahoma City in a Pierce Arrow touring car with a chauffeur. Courtesy Oklahoma Publishing Company.

Governor Murray did not eat desserts and liked plain food, simply prepared with only a little salt. He liked his biscuits raw in the center. Once he fired a mansion cook who could not master his instructions to brown the outside but leave the middle portion of biscuits uncooked. Mrs. Murray enjoyed assisting the mansion cook in meal preparation. Her husband believed eating onions gave him mental prowess. He could make a meal of a leafy salad topped with chopped onions, with cornbread and buttermilk on the side.

The first lady's Indian heritage was evident in the furnishings of the mansion. Above a large portrait of Governor Murray hung an Indian peace pipe and wampum belt, the gift of Chief Millet Hoy Koy Bitty of the Comanches. The Chief had offered a peace prayer of the red man at Murray's inauguration.

Because of the shortage of state funds to improve the lot of the governor's mansion, Mrs. Murray used her own money to buy additional flowers and shrubs. She planted rare Bolivian plants from seeds she had brought from her husband's previous attempts at establishing colonies of Oklahomans in Bolivia.

Early in their administration, Mrs. Murray hosted a dance at the governor's mansion to honor their daughter. The Christmas-season dance found the mansion's spiral stairway entwined with greenery while about the rooms were vases and bowls of red blossoms, holly wreaths, poinsettias, and other reminders of the holiday season. The ballroom on the third floor was a "bower of southern smilax with two Christmas trees gaily decorated." The dance was reportedly the first time the mansion was opened for "the young folk." Jean Murray and friend Alvin Pickens led the grand march to kick off the festivities. The first lady served "supper" at midnight in the dining room.

On another occasion, Governor Murray found teenagers sitting in the ballroom, in his opinion, too close to each other. He loudly announced the mansion was not a bawdy house and put an end to mansion parties to which young people were welcome. Couples were welcome at the mansion only if the men brought their own wives. As "Alfalfa Bill" put it, "The society in the mansion shall include only those who come to the mansion with their own wife."

One of Mrs. Murray's least favorite and least stately functions as first lady was to place newspapers around the governor's bed to protect the floor from his frequent spitting of tobacco juice.

When springtime came the first lady worked in the mansion rose garden. She suggested placing a marker by the many perennials that have been given to the first family by residents of the state's 77 counties.

Only one of the Murray's five children, Jean, age 22, moved to the mansion with her parents when her father was elected governor. Four sons, Burbank; William, Jr.; Massena; and Johnston, later a governor of Oklahoma; had established their own homes before their father was elected.

The governor's mansion was completely open to the public during the Murray administration. Mrs. Murray believed the mansion belonged to the people and she was just the caretaker. Whoever came to the mansion, be it the curious or the friendly, was welcome. Even if the governor refused to see someone calling at the mansion, the first lady made the visitor welcome and listened to any cause or complaint with a sympathetic ear.

Mrs. Murray did not make herself become the governor's mansion, she made the mansion become her. She had a certain canny sense, a perceptive quality, whimsical but definitive.

Governor Murray was considered by many to be eccentric. He chained chairs to radiators in his office to prevent guests from pulling them closer to his desk, a move to prevent the spread of germs. The lone exception was when old friend Will Rogers came to the governor's office. Murray had a chair brought in for the famed Oklahoma humorist. The two "characters" would sit for hours and tell stories while snacking on cheese and crackers.

Murray called out the national guard 27 times and declared martial law on 34 occasions. Among his reasons for using the national guard were to prevent the legislature from meeting and to defy a federal judge's decision allowing a toll bridge to span the Red River south of Durant. However, "Alfalfa Bill" 's most eccentric move may have been his decision on the use of the land surrounding the governor's mansion.

In 1932 Murray ordered groundskeepers to stop mowing the mansion lawn. Within weeks wild oats and weeds were half a man tall. When asked about the condition of the mansion lawn, the crusty "Alfalfa Bill" said he was growing chicken feed and would soon harvest the crop. Murray, worried about his unemployed neighbors on Northeast 23rd Street, allocated a half-acre each to ten needy families to grow potatoes. Soon the lush green lawn that had been manicured to perfection during the Holloway years in the mansion was plowed and planted with seed potatoes.

Even though Murray may be best remembered for his eccentricities, he was a strong governor who guided Oklahoma through some of its poorest years. During his administration the Oklahoma Tax Commission was created to give Oklahoma a solid tax base to support state services. Murray's populist views caught on across America. He was an active candidate for the Democratic presidential nomination in 1932, eventually losing to Franklin D. Roosevelt.

Mrs. Murray was well liked by many Oklahomans because of her willingness to answer the mansion door any time for some poor mother who sought help from the governor for an imprisoned son. She also prepared sandwiches for her husband's late-night meetings with legislators and other state officials. She mainly stayed out of political

First Lady Alice Murray working in the mansion garden in August, 1933. Mrs. Murray cared deeply about the appearance of the mansion grounds and worked to plant flowers and shrubs to beautify the official residence of the governor. Courtesy Oklahoma Publishing Company.

Jean Murray, left, admires one of her mother's paintings. First Lady Alice Murray was a gifted artist who spent long hours at the mansion with brush in hand. Courtesy Oklahoma Publishing Company.

Facing page: Governor William H. "Alfalfa Bill" Murray, First Lady Alice Murray, and daughter Jean Murray prepare to vacate the governor's mansion, January 13, 1935. All of their personal items had been packed for shipment to Broken Bow where Murray had purchased 37 acres on Yashua Creek for a new family home. Courtesy Oklahoma Publishing Company.

First Lady Alice Murray sliced bread as she prepared a late night snack for legislative leaders visiting the governor's mansion in 1932. Courtesy Oklahoma Publishing Company.

affairs. She would have liked to live in the mansion another four years but the state constitution, at the time, prohibited a governor from succeeding himself. The only time Mrs. Murray entered the political arena was to urge her husband to run for governor again in 1938 so she might spend her 40th wedding anniversary in the mansion. However, Murray's re-election attempt was unsuccessful.

When Mrs. Murray died August 28, 1938, her body lay in state in the Blue Room of the State Capitol, the first wife of a governor to be so honored. Governor E.W. Marland, even though a political enemy of "Alfalfa Bill," offered the governor's mansion as a place for Mrs. Murray's body to be seen by well-wishers. However, the recalcitrant Murray declined the offer, opting instead for his beloved wife's body to lie in state in the Capitol.

From around the state came messages of sympathy. Murray's own "Adios, Alice, Adieu," written a week after her death, revealed the depth of his love for his wife. She was his ideal of a good wife, one who managed the home, reared the children, and always remained apart from her husband's political life. He praised her for the way she had brought up the children and kept the mansion. Governor Murray was unable to accept his wife's death and later referred to her as if she were still alive.

In his last years, Governor Murray lived at the Roberts Hotel in downtown Oklahoma City where he often gave "statesmanship" lessons to his grandchildren. Grandson William H. Murray, III, nicknamed "Bino" by his famous grandfather, spent Sunday afternoons listening to the former governor impart his wisdom on the importance of poetry, public speaking, and politics.

Governor Murray died October 15, 1956, a month before his 87th birthday. He lived long enough to see his son, Johnston, elected governor of Oklahoma.

For more information on the William H. Murray family, see:

Fischer, LeRoy H., editor. *Oklahoma's Governors: 1929 to 1955 Depression to Prosperity* (Oklahoma City: Oklahoma Historical Society, 1983)

Bryant, Keith L. *Alfalfa Bill Murray* (Norman: University of Oklahoma Press, 1968)

Kenneth D. Hendrickson, editor. *Hard Times in Oklahoma: The Depression Years* (Oklahoma City: Oklahoma Historical Society, 1983)

Hines, Gordon. *Alfalfa Bill Murray, An Intimate Biography* (Oklahoma City: Oklahoma Press, 1932)

Murray, William H. *Memoirs of Governor Murray and True History of Oklahoma* (Boston: Meador Publishing Company, 1945)

Ernest Whitworth Marland is said to have won and lost a $100 million fortune. He built an oil company that became Conoco. He was the victim of one of the country's earliest corporate takeovers. He tragically died a short time after leaving the governor's mansion. Courtesy Oklahoma Historical Society.

The discovery of oil changed the looks of the grounds of the governor's mansion and adjacent state-owned property. Courtesy Oklahoma Historical Society

A MYSTICAL FIRST LADY

MARLAND was born May 8, 1874, in Pennsylvania and practiced law in his home state before entering the oil exploration business. He came to Oklahoma in 1908 with not much more than a belief in himself and a small letter of credit. He became president of the Marland Oil Company, which later became Conoco, one of the nation's largest oil companies. Marland was an oil gambler who won and lost a fortune of nearly $100 million. At one time in his career Marland controlled nearly one-tenth of the world's oil production.

Marland served Oklahoma well during his public career. He was a member of Congress for one term before he was elected governor in 1934. As governor he promoted the development of the Oklahoma Highway Patrol and the Interstate Oil and Gas Compact Commission. However, he suffered setbacks in attempts to carry out an economic recovery program due to a disagreement with the legislature over the

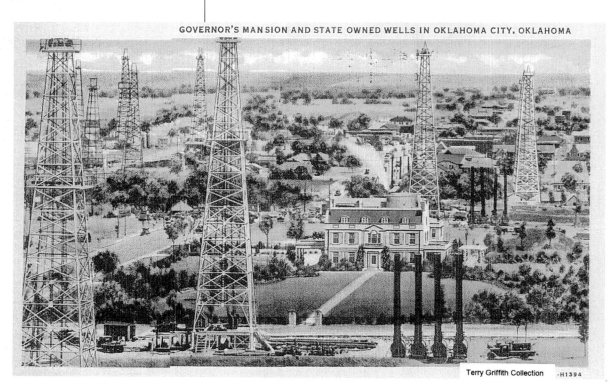

GOVERNOR'S MANSION AND STATE OWNED WELLS IN OKLAHOMA CITY, OKLAHOMA

Terry Griffith Collection -H1394

nature of government's role in taxation. Marland's efforts brought relief and hope to many and started Oklahoma on the road to recovery. At one time 90,000 Oklahomans were working on more than 1,300 Works Progress Administration (WPA) projects.

Lydie Roberts Marland, usually known as Lyde, or Princess Lyde, born in Pennsylvania on April 7, 1900, became first lady of Oklahoma in an unusual way. She was the niece of Governor Marland's first wife, Virginia, who had been an invalid for many years before she died in 1926. Marland and Virginia had no children of their own so they invited her sister's two children, George and Lydie, to live with them in Ponca City. Eventually, the Marlands adopted the two children. Lydie, from age 16, served as the official hostess at parties and other special events in the Marland home. Lydie was well educated by the Marlands and attended eastern boarding schools. She traveled abroad and was an accomplished dancer and horsewoman.

In 1928, the year the Marland Mansion was completed in Ponca City, Marland and his adopted daughter, Lydie, traveled in his private railcar to Pennsylvania so the adoption could be annulled and they could be married. The girl who had been his niece, his daughter, and now his wife received the completed elaborate Marland Mansion as a wedding gift. Called the

Lydie Marland arrives at the governor's mansion in January, 1935, to assume her role as first lady of Oklahoma. Courtesy Oklahoma Publishing Company.

Princess Lyde, as
Oklahomans called her,
descends the spiral staircase
in the governor's mansion,
January 15, 1935. Courtesy
Oklahoma Publishing
Company.

"scandal that shocked the nation," newspaper tabloids across the country jumped on the story of the 54-year-old millionaire marrying the beautiful 28-year-old woman who had been his daughter for the previous 12 years.

The Marland Mansion was something to behold. The magnificent Italian villa had 55 rooms, 15 baths, and 3 complete kitchens. Florentine murals graced the walls. Waterford crystal chandeliers hung in the ballroom and dining room. The grounds contained three lakes, a polo field, a large swimming pool, and lavish Hampton Court style gardens. Prominent in the garden was a sculpture of Lydie. Later, after Governor Marland's death, Lydie ordered the sculpture destroyed. However, in 1990, the statue was discovered where it had been buried for 40 years. It has been restored and now stands in the Marland Mansion's foyer.

A few months after they were married, Marland was in financial ruin and was ousted from his company by New York City's J. P.

Lydie Marland in the mansion library. On weekends, the first family often traveled to Ponca City where they were joined by such friends as Will Rogers for polo matches, fox hunts, and jazz parties. Lydie was well read and accomplished in the social graces. Courtesy Oklahoma Historical Society.

The mansion living room or library during the Marland administration. Most of the original furnishings of the room were still in place a decade after the mansion was first occupied by the Johnstons. Courtesy Oklahoma Publishing Company.

Left: The mansion dining room during the Marland administration. The furniture was original, only the chair cushions had changed. Note the Marland silver service on the buffet that had been brought to the mansion from the Marland Mansion in Ponca City. Courtesy Oklahoma Publishing Company.

Below: Against one wall of the main hall or foyer stood a solid walnut console, hand carved with an Italian marble top. That piece of furniture and the wall mirror are two of only a few items that remained in the mansion over the years. Courtesy Oklahoma Publishing Company.

Lydie Marland's bedroom at the governor's mansion was furnished with furniture from the Marland Mansion in Ponca City. Today, the bed is displayed with the same bedspread at the Marland Mansion. Courtesy Oklahoma Publishing Company.

Morgan Bank in one of the country's earliest hostile takeovers. He and his new bride moved to the cottage behind the Marland Mansion because he could not afford the $800 monthly electric bill for the sprawling mansion.

In January, 1935, a lengthy inaugural parade wound around the streets of Oklahoma City on its way to the State Capitol for the Marland inauguration. A military band was followed by a troop of cavalry from the Oklahoma Military Academy. Decorated cars and elaborate floats were entered in the parade by cities, towns, counties, and civic organizations.

Hand clapping and yelling broke out along the parade route as the governor's light blue, open car passed. The governor, a "picture of satisfaction" as his blue eyes gleamed through spectacles tinted slightly pink, lifted his hat and smiled, waving the "topper" around the panorama. The top hat was so in demand for the inaugural activities that Oklahoma City clothing stores reported there was not one top hat left in the capital city for purchase by inauguration eve. The top hat worn by Governor Marland at his inauguration was in stark contrast to "Alfalfa Bill" Murray's falling socks and old muffler four years before.

"Youthfully regal" aptly described first lady Lydie Marland at the inaugural ball. Dressed in a backless, velvet gown, Mrs. Marland hosted a lavish State Capitol party for thousands of men in tails and top hats and women in sequins as an air of aristocracy returned to the governor's office.

Cowboys with boots, spurs, and ten-gallon hats stood near Indians clutching their blankets and other Native Americans in buckskin. Jazz bands played torrid tunes on three floors of the Capitol. Crowds of small boys and clusters of well-dressed adults crashed through hordes of people jammed in Capitol hallways.

An antique piano enhanced the décor of the music room. The Henry Johnstons planned to buy a piano for the governor's mansion but never did so. Subsequent governors were forced to furnish their own piano for the music room. Courtesy Oklahoma Publishing Company.

GOVERNOR'S MANSION, OKLAHOMA CITY, OKLAHOMA

Governor Marland's Japanese gardener oversaw the planting of ivy to soften the walls of the governor's mansion. Courtesy Oklahoma Historical Society.

Streams of dignitaries and common folk passed through the reception line where Governor and Mrs. Marland stood gracefully into the night. Lincoln Boulevard twinkled with lights of moving cars as thousands danced and sang past midnight.

Using decorating experience gained during the construction of the Marland Mansion, Lydie began redecorating the governor's mansion immediately upon moving into the official residence in 1935. She carpeted the upstairs of the mansion and moved many pieces of furniture and wall hangings from her home in Ponca City. More than $1,000 was spent on repairing damaged walls.

The mansion's redecorated state dining room was described in an April, 1936, newspaper story as "decorated in gold and green. Jade green silk damask draperies blend with the gold net glass curtains. Green and gold shades and designs appear in the chenille rug—Walnut paneling extends seven feet upon the walls around the room and tapestry is employed on the surface above."

Truckloads of magnificent evergreens and shrubs were transplanted to the mansion grounds from the Marland Mansion. Landscaping was important to Governor Marland whose influence and employment of a Japanese gardener caused Ponca City to be one of the most beautifully landscaped cities in the Southwest.

Oil was discovered underneath the governor's mansion in 1935. Governor Marland, experienced in oil exploration, was the perfect man to be in the governor's mansion to develop the state's oil reserves.

The British American Oil Producing Company drilled the Pearson No. 1 well that produced 27,000 barrels of oil in 24 hours. Residents of neighborhoods around the mansion and State Capitol strongly objected to Governor Marland allowing oil production, prompting a legal and philosophical battle between Oklahoma City and Marland over the drilling of oil wells on state property. The City contended its zoning laws could control all activities within its corporate limits, even on state property. However, Marland won the battle and ordered state militia to protect drillers on state property. At one time there were 24 oil wells pumping simultaneously from beneath the State Capitol and mansion grounds, literally pumping millions of dollars into state coffers.

After Marland left the governor's office, he returned to Ponca City to try to reorganize the Marland Oil Company. He was unsuccessful in two campaigns for the United States Senate. One of his Senate campaigns was in the middle of his term as governor, the other in 1938. He also unsuccessfully tried to regain his congressional seat in 1940. He died a broken man on October 3, 1941, in the chauffeur's quarters, now called Lydie's cottage, of the Marland Mansion.

After her husband's death, Lydie lived a reclusive life in Ponca City until she loaded her 1948 Studebaker with paintings, tapestries, and $10,000 in cash, and disappeared in 1953. The *Saturday Evening Post* published an article entitled "Where is Lydie Marland?" The Oklahoma State Bureau of Investigation entered the case, looking for the former first lady who drove around the country without a driver's license. Her vision was so defective she required a magnifying glass to read a newspaper.

 In August, 1955, Lydie's brother George reported her as officially missing. She was located cleaning rooms at the Moonlight Motel in Independence, Missouri. Dressed in Indian maiden clothes, she made beds in the motel. She shied away from rooms occupied by guests with Oklahoma license plates.

Oklahoma law enforcement officers closed their file, finding no evidence of foul play. They concluded that Lydie had the right to hide from her past. However, Lydie kept the taxes paid on her Ponca City property left to her by her husband.

Lydie lived in Kansas City, Missouri, on the West Coast, and near Central Park in New York City before she was found by Ponca City attorney C. D. Northcutt in 1975. He loaned her money to return to Ponca City. She was 75 years old, destitute, toothless, and lonely. She moved back into the cottage on the Marland Mansion grounds and lived there until her death at the age of 87 on July 25, 1987. She existed on a small pension from Conoco paid to the widow of the former chairman of the board of the company. Only six persons attended Lydie's funeral. The only flowers came from Conoco.

Historian Glenda Carlile described Lydie's final years in Ponca City, "In the very early evenings just before dusk, the residents of Ponca City

The restored statue of First Lady Lydie Marland now graces the foyer of the Marland Mansion in Ponca City. Courtesy Marland Mansion.

were accustomed to seeing a shadowy figure stroll the streets. On closer inspection it was a woman wearing a long black dress over black and green checked pants, faded tennis shoes, a dark hat, and an old scarf. The small body was stooped forward staring at the street in front of her, not speaking to anyone who passed by—the people respected her privacy and her desire to be left alone. They remembered another time when Lyde Marland had reigned supreme over Ponca City and when she was the first lady of the State of Oklahoma."

Lydie's relationship with her late husband was the topic of books, magazine articles, and countless newspaper stories. However, her opinion of E.W. Marland, and her brother, George, was succinctly characterized by her comments, often overheard by friends and acquaintances in Ponca City. Lydie said, "Oh, I miss my men so much."

For more information on the E.W. Marland family, see:

Apman, Patti. *Lyde Roberts Marland, the Princess of the Palace on the Prairie* (Ponca City: Marland Mansion, 1995)

Mathews, John Joseph. *Life and Death of an Oilman: The Career of E.W. Marland* (Norman: University of Oklahoma Press, 1951)

Franks, Kenny A., Paul F. Lambert, and Carl N. Tyson. *Early Oklahoma Oil* (College Station: Texas A & M Press, 1981)

Wade, Henry F. *Ship of State on a Sea of Oil* (Oklahoma City: privately printed, 1972)

Carlile, Glenda. *Petticoats, Politics, and Pirouette* (Oklahoma City, Southern Hills Publishing Company, 1995)

The Marland Mansion in Ponca City is on the National Register of Historic Places. This magnificent mansion reflects the elegance of the affluent E.W. Marland who lived lavishly and entertained in the same style. It was designed and constructed as a showplace for pieces of fine art and in the process it became a masterpiece in its own right. It was called the "Palace on the Prairie." Courtesy Oklahoma Publishing Company.

Leon C. "Red" Phillips served as Speaker of the Oklahoma House of Representatives before he was elected governor in 1938. Courtesy Oklahoma Historical Society.

The first family in 1939. Left to right, Lois Ann Phillips, Governor Leon C. "Red" Phillips, First Lady Myrtle Phillips, and Robert Rowe "Bob" Phillips. Courtesy Western History Collection, University of Oklahoma.

WHEN LEON CHASE "RED" PHILLIPS WAS INAUGURATED AS GOVERNOR OF OKLAHOMA IN 1939, HE AND FIRST LADY MYRTLE PHILLIPS MOVED INTO THE MANSION WITH 12-YEAR-OLD LOIS ANN. THE PHILLIPS' 16-YEAR-OLD SON ROBERT ROWE WAS ALLOWED TO STAY IN OKEMAH TO COMPLETE HIGH SCHOOL.

A TEENAGER IN THE MANSION

GOVERNOR PHILLIPS was born December 9, 1890, in Missouri but moved to Oklahoma at an early age. He studied for the ministry at Oklahoma City's Epworth University, later Oklahoma City University, but changed to law and graduated from the University of Oklahoma in 1916.

Phillips planned to marry Myrtle Ellenberger of Norman on June 7, 1916, on the same day he was to receive his law degree and medal as all-around student at the University of Oklahoma. However, severe abdominal pains waylaid all plans for June 7. The future governor was loaded onto a baggage car on the interurban to be transported to St. Anthony's Hospital in Oklahoma City for surgery. After 12 days in the hospital, Phillips insisted upon being released. He called an ambulance and was taken to the Supreme Court office and was sworn in to practice law. From there he went to Norman, and, supporting his emaciated body with a cane, was married to Myrtle. Two days later the young

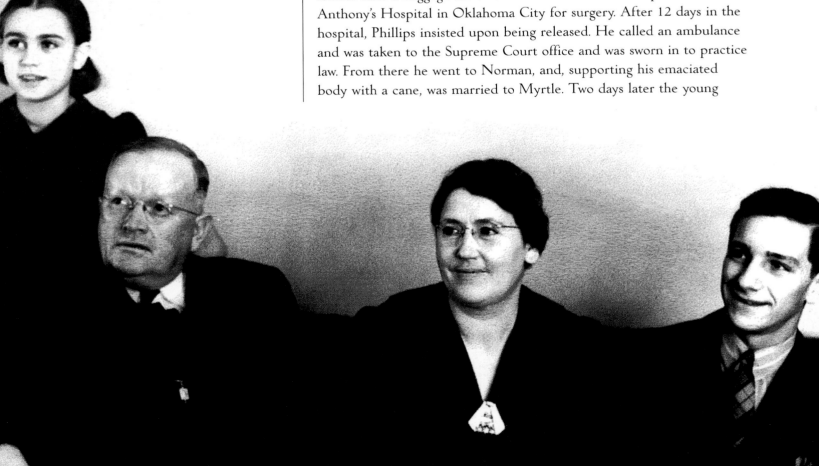

couple went "flat broke" to Okemah with Phillips' desire to establish a small town law practice.

Phillips was elected to the Oklahoma House of Representatives in 1932 and established himself as a dynamic and forceful member of the House. He was chosen by Governor Marland as Speaker of the House in 1935. Promising sweeping cuts in government and relief for the needy, he was elected governor in 1938. Under his guidance, the state accumulated a $5 million surplus.

Phillips battled the federal government continuously during his administration. He resented the growing role of the government in Washington, D.C. He believed that Oklahomans should be allowed to control their natural resources without interference from the federal government. He also battled the federal government over the construction of Lake Texhoma. Literally hating the New Deal policies of President Franklin D. Roosevelt, Phillips bolted from the Democratic Party in 1942 during the final months of his term as governor. He later rejoined the party.

Governor Leon C. "Red" Phillips and First Lady Myrtle Phillips leave the Blue Room at the State Capitol with a national guard escort to lead the Grand March around the second floor rotunda starting the inaugural ball in January, 1939. Courtesy Oklahoma Publishing Company.

Lois Ann Phillips admires a map made of Oklahoma stone from each county given to Governor Phillips by the Oklahoma Highway Patrol in 1941. Courtesy Lois Ann Phillips Berndt.

First Lady Myrtle Phillips made her daughter Lois Ann a priority. The first lady and governor spent a great deal of time making certain Lois Ann's life was as normal as possible even though she lived in the governor's mansion. Courtesy Oklahoma Publishing Company.

First Lady Myrtle Phillips on the mansion spiral staircase. The reception hall wallpaper was a brown French toile. Mrs. Phillips was proud of the official residence and often invited friends and civic groups to hold their meetings in the mansion. Courtesy Oklahoma Publishing Company.

Governor Phillips made a lasting contribution to the budgeting process in state government. In 1941 he publicly supported State Question 298, an amendment to the state constitution that required a balanced budget, limiting expenditures to the amount of available income.

Myrtle Faye Phillips was a quiet, gracious, and amiable first lady. She was born in Iowa November 22, 1891, the only girl in a family of five children. Her parents moved to a farm near Norman in 1901. She graduated Phi Beta Kappa from the University of Oklahoma in 1912.

A mile-long parade kicked off the Phillips' inaugural festivities in January, 1939. National guard units and the University of Oklahoma marching band led the parade that featured a dozen bands and the Okemah Buckaroos, red-shirted cowboys from Governor Phillips' hometown of Okemah.

After the inauguration, the Phillips hosted friends and family in the State Capitol Blue Room and later led the grand march around the second floor rotunda to officially begin the inaugural ball. The governor sported his signature cigar while Mrs. Phillips gleamed in a long sequined dress. Robert Phillips' companion for the evening was Imogene Storms of Okemah, later the wife of Oklahoma Congressman Glen D. Johnson, Sr., and mother of Oklahoma House Speaker and Southeastern Oklahoma State University President Glen D. Johnson, Jr.

Living in the mansion was anything but pleasant for Lois Ann Phillips as she entered her teenage years. It was difficult for her to adjust to living under the label of "governor's daughter" after growing up in the small town of Okemah. She brought her German Shepherd,

First Lady Myrtle Phillips in the sunroom of the mansion reading the latest issue of a favorite magazine. Some historians have written that the sunroom was once a screened-in porch. However, photographs such as this prove that the sunroom was always a fully enclosed room of the mansion. Courtesy Oklahoma Publishing Company.

First Lady Myrtle Phillips shows off her modern kitchen in the mansion. Mrs. Phillips loved to entertain friends, especially her former neighbors from Okemah. Courtesy Oklahoma Publishing

By 1939 the shrubs around the governor's mansion were large and obscured the face of the limestone structure. Courtesy Oklahoma Historical Society.

Barney, to the mansion. However, Barney dug under the mansion fence and was killed by a car on Northeast 23rd Street. He was the first of many pets to be buried on the mansion grounds.

The governor and first lady installed a ping-pong table and shuffleboard court in the mansion basement to make the official residence more teenager friendly. When Lois Ann was elected football queen her junior year at Oklahoma City Central High School, the Phillips hosted a dinner for the football team and coaches at the mansion. After dinner the guests previewed a new movie, *My Gal Sal*, starring Rita Hayworth and Victor Mature.

After they left the governor's mansion, Governor and Mrs. Phillips were divorced. She was an active member of St. Luke's United Methodist Church in Oklahoma City where she was president of Vaught's Sunday School Class. She was also a member of a philanthropic educational organization (PEO). She died June 23, 1961. Governor Phillips died while practicing law in Okmulgee March 27, 1958.

For more information on the Leon C. Phillips family, see:

Fischer, LeRoy H., editor. *Oklahoma's Governors, 1929-1955 Depression to Prosperity*

(Oklahoma City: Oklahoma Historical Society, 1983)

A panoramic view of the State Capitol east to the governor's mansion ca. 1939. Oil wells dotted the horizon. Note the street car in the lower right hand portion of the photograph. Courtesy Oklahoma Historical Society.

Governor Robert S. Kerr poses with a barrel of molasses and a sack of pecans as part of his wager with the governor of Nebraska that Oklahomans could sell more war bonds in 1943. Courtesy Oklahoma Publishing Company.

AMERICA WAS IN THE GRIPS OF WORLD WAR II, AND OKLAHOMA WAS EMERGING FROM THE SCARS OF THE GREAT DEPRESSION AND DUST BOWL DAYS WHEN ROBERT SAMUEL KERR WAS ELECTED GOVERNOR IN 1942.

A
KING
IN THE
MAKING

THE AUSTERE ATMOSPHERE prevented the Kerrs from having an inaugural ball, even though Oklahomans' spirits were raised with Kerr's election and hope for a better and more prosperous decade for the Sooner State. Kerr was on his way to being elected to the United States Senate and ultimately becoming the uncrowned king of the Senate.

Kerr was the first governor to be born in what would become the State of Oklahoma. He entered the world in a log cabin near Ada in Indian Territory, September 11, 1896. Kerr practiced law in Ada before launching into the oil business with his brother Aubrey Kerr. His

The front entrance to the governor's mansion in May, 1945. Note the awnings and shrubs that reached almost to the third floor of the executive residence. Courtesy Oklahoma Historical Society.

ventures with Dean A. McGee created Kerr-McGee Corporation, one of Oklahoma's most successful oil companies. Kerr often said, "I'm just like you, only I struck oil."

As governor, Kerr liquidated the state debt of $44 million and amassed a $40 million surplus. He took advantage of revenues newly created by wartime prosperity to increase state funding for schools, highways, and public health. Yet, he resisted attempts by the legislature to reduce taxes, and he maintained a balanced budget. He also recognized the state's potential for postwar expansion and supported laws to encourage economic development. As an ardent Democrat and faithful supporter of President Franklin D. Roosevelt, Kerr became well known throughout the nation as the keynote speaker at Democratic functions.

Grayce Breene Kerr was born in Ohio in 1901. Her father was an oil man who moved his family to Bartlesville, Oklahoma, when Grayce was in high school. She was a gifted pianist and soprano who envisioned a career in opera. However, a visit to her sister's home in Ada in

The Kerr family in the southwest living room, or library, on the first floor of the mansion. Left to right, Kay Kerr, Governor Kerr, Bill Kerr, Breene Kerr, First Lady Grayce Kerr, and Robert S. Kerr, Jr. Courtesy Kay Kerr Adair.

Right: First Lady Grayce Kerr, center, often entertained service women in the sunroom at the mansion during World War II. Courtesy Robert S. Kerr Museum, Poteau, Oklahoma.

Below: Governor Robert S. Kerr and daughter Kay playing with three of the family dogs on the mansion grounds in 1945. The Kerrs children always had several dogs for pets. Courtesy Kay Kerr Adair.

September, 1925, changed her life. While singing at the Ada Lions Club, she sat beside the program chairman, a big, young lawyer named Robert S. Kerr. He loved to tell the story of seeing the tall blonde girl playing tennis and his decision on the spot that she was the girl he wanted to marry. After a whirlwind romance they were married the day after Christmas. It was Kerr's second marriage.

After Kerr was inaugurated in January, 1943, he and members of his family greeted thousands of Oklahomans in a two-hour Blue Room reception at the State Capitol. Exhausted women staggered into the first available chairs to ease their aching feet after the ordeal of standing in line. The new governor, his wife, and mother stood up well under the punishment, "smiling to the end." A reporter observed, "The Kerrs are rugged people."

The new first lady was shy and her primary focus in life was her husband and children. The governor's mansion during the Kerr years was filled with laughter. Mrs. Kerr spent most of her waking hours overseeing the lives of her four children, Robert S, Kerr, Jr., 16; Breene Kerr, 14; Kay Kerr, 12; and William Graycen Kerr, 5.

Having three teenagers in the mansion was an interesting experience. The Kerr children brought several dogs with them to their new home. Family dogs were important to the Kerrs. All kinds of dogs, mostly without pedigree, lived inside and outside the mansion.

Kay Kerr Adair remembered the "storybook house with a sweeping circular staircase." The many rooms on both floors were spacious for the most part, except a cubby hole bedroom on the northeast corner of the second floor which her brother Breene occupied and which was adjacent to a small back stairway down to the kitchen and basement.

Kay recalled a small guard room adjacent to the front entry of the mansion where "a kindly old man," the mansion guard, sat for hours, listening to the radio, and spinning yarns to the children when they came home from school. It was in that room that Kay heard the radio announcing the death of Franklin Roosevelt and later the end of the war in Europe.

While Kay Kerr was recuperating from emergency surgery, First Lady Grayce Kerr repapered Kay's bedroom, complete with peonies on the ceiling. In subsequent administrations, the windows in this room were closed and closets were added on either side of the fireplace. Courtesy Oklahoma Publishing Company.

The Kerr's youngest son, Bill, and the family's St. Bernard in the mansion library. Courtesy Kay Kerr Adair.

First Lady Grayce Kerr, left, and Kay Kerr relax in the mansion library, 1945. Courtesy Oklahoma Publishing Company.

Rare snow covered the mansion grounds in the winter of 1945. Courtesy Robert S. Kerr Museum, Poteau, Oklahoma.

Grayce Kerr and the mansion kitchen staff always made certain that the Kerr children had access to the kitchen. After school nourishment was usually peanut butter and jelly. On special occasions, trays of cookies and sandwiches left over from some formal function and a large kettle of hot spiced tea awaited the Kerr children.

The mansion kitchen was a center of activity for the Kerrs. Kay Kerr described her family's love for food, "Our mother enjoyed cooking and our family were big eaters in a sort of combined style of gourmet cooking (our mother's way) and farmhouse spread (our dad's way)."

When Robert S. Kerr, Jr., was off at war, there was a mansion dining room chair purposely left empty for Christmas dinner, signifying that the Kerr family was not complete.

Often first lady duties took Grayce Kerr from the kitchen, and a trustee from the state penitentiary in McAlester assumed the responsibility of preparing meals for the Kerr family. Coy Brown sang in the kitchen while he worked. Brown, who later served as presiding state bishop over the Church of God in Christ, married while working in the mansion. He and his wife Thelma moved into the second-story apartment of the mansion garage.

Grayce Kerr placed her grand piano in the music room and was often overheard working off the tensions of the day playing and singing Sigmond Romberg and other light opera pieces.

Governor Kerr gave much of the credit for his success to the first lady. He called her "My Grayce." When he was referred to as a self-made man, he often replied, "No, I'm a wife-made man."

Because Bob and Grayce Kerr did not dance, the ballroom on the third floor of the mansion was largely unused during the Kerr administration except as a hideout for the children and a great roller-skating rink for Kay Kerr. The strong religious convictions endorsed by the Kerrs also prohibited the presence of alcoholic beverages in the mansion. Governor Kerr was a staunch Baptist, and Mrs. Kerr was active in the First Church of Christ Scientist.

When Kay was 13, she was hospitalized for emergency surgery for appendicitis. When she returned home, the first lady had repapered Kay's bedroom, including the ceiling, with a bright floral paper. While recuperating, Kay was given a new dog, a Toy Spitz, named Magnolia, who became a favorite of Governor Kerr. Often Magnolia was lowered in a basket to waiting friends from Kay's second-floor bedroom. Magnolia did not seem to mind the elaborate engineering feat.

After his term as governor, Kerr was elected to the United States Senate and became one of America's most powerful leaders. His efforts changed much of Oklahoma's landscape. His leadership resulted in the McClellan-Kerr Arkansas River Navigation System. One historian said, "If Bob Kerr could have lived long enough, the Red River would be navigable." Kerr also was a major figure in America's successful space race to the moon. When he died at age 66 on January 1, 1963, *The Daily Oklahoman* wrote, "A giant has fallen. Oklahoma's ablest and most honored native son was struck down yesterday—No other man had fought so hard and achieved so much in raising Oklahoma to a high place in the eyes of the world."

While living in Washington, D.C., where her husband served in the United States Senate, Mrs. Kerr opened an interior decorating shop in Georgetown and began collecting and selling antiques.

While building a new home near Poteau, Mrs. Kerr operated the Black Angus Restaurant, known for its Angus burgers and hot apple pie with rum sauce. The rum flavor was provided by artificial means because Senator Kerr did not condone the use of rum. Mrs. Kerr had managed a big household when her husband was governor and United States Senator and had served meals to as many as 20 or 30 people. She said running a restaurant would not be so different from her previous life's work; so she set about building a reputation for her chicken fried steaks, pies, hot rolls, and Angus burgers.

The Kerr's sprawling ranch home was perched atop a green-forested hill near Poteau. The home reflected Mrs. Kerr's interior decorating expertise. The Robert S. Kerr Museum is now located in the former Kerr home, which also is operated as a bed and breakfast.

Mrs. Kerr later married Olney Flynn, a childhood friend who was a Tulsa oil man and Republican gubernatorial candidate in 1946. The former first lady died of cancer in 1965 at age 64 after spending several months in a Christian Scientist sanitarium in Colorado. Mrs. Kerr had been a strong advocate of Christian Science beliefs for most of her life.

For more information on the Robert S. Kerr family, see:

Morgan, Anne Hodges. *Robert S. Kerr, The Senate Years* (Norman: University of Oklahoma Press, 1977)

Kerr, Robert S. *Land, Wood, and Water* (New York: Fleet Publishing Corporation, 1960)

Top: First Lady Grayce Kerr decorating the mansion Christmas tree in December, 1945. Courtesy Oklahoma Publishing Company.

Bottom: First Lady Grayce Kerr was able to draw upon the Kerr personal fortune to make the governor's mansion a more livable home. She moved much of her personal furniture into the upstairs of the executive residence to mask the fading finery. Courtesy Oklahoma Publishing Company.

After Roy J. Turner was governor he served on the Oklahoma Highway Commission and as treasurer of the Democratic National Committee. Courtesy Oklahoma Publishing Company.

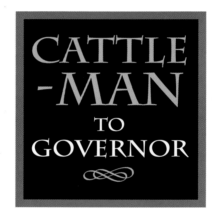

CATTLE -MAN TO GOVERNOR

TURNER, born November 5, 1894, in Lincoln County, Oklahoma Territory, purchased the Turner Ranch in 1933 and began developing one of the world's finest Hereford cattle operations. One of the bulls produced from his herd became the world's first million-dollar bull.

While Turner dabbled in real estate and oil, his primary focus during the 1930s and early 1940s was the Turner Ranch. The Turner family, including twins, Bill and Betty, adopted when they were four weeks old, maintained their official residence in Oklahoma City where Turner served on the Board of Education from 1939 to 1946 when he was elected governor. Mrs. Turner, the former Jessica Grimm, was active in charitable organizations and served on the Oklahoma City Library Board.

Turner was inaugurated January 13, 1947. The new first lady selected a gold, street-length dress for the inauguration and reception at the Blue Room of the State Capitol. She wore a small, frilly hat and an orchid.

Turner was a songwriter, penning *Hereford Heaven*, his official campaign song in 1946. Turner sang with his quartet at the inaugural, making him the only Oklahoma governor ever to sing at his own inauguration.

Mrs. Turner, 20 years younger than her husband, welcomed the responsibility of maintaining two homes, one at the governor's mansion and the other at "Hereford Heaven," the common name for the Turner Ranch.

The twins were 19 when their father was elected. Mrs. Turner's mother, Etta L. Grimm, also lived at the governor's mansion. The Turners were served by one cook, one maid, three guards, two yardmen, and a laundress, all on a budget of $6,000 appropriated by the legislature for annual support of the mansion staff.

First Lady Jessica Turner, center, serves soft drinks to students from Oklahoma City's Classen High School. Mrs. Turner welcomed students to the mansion. She wanted her children to live a near-normal life and believed that constant contact with students their own age would prevent them from becoming isolated as the children of the governor. Courtesy Oklahoma Publishing Company.

The Turner family at their
southern Oklahoma ranch.
Left to right, Betty Turner,
First Lady Jessica Turner, Bill
Turner, and Governor Roy
Turner. The Turners spent
more time at the ranch
than at the governor's
mansion. Courtesy
Oklahoma Publishing
Company.

When the Turners moved into the mansion in January, 1947, the
furniture was in bad shape. First Lady Jessica Turner asked Chet Smith,
Capitol custodian, to store the worn-out furniture while she moved
newer furniture into four bedrooms and the mansion living room from
the ranch house in Sulphur. Mrs. Turner supervised some minor
repainting and redecorating of the mansion. The governor told
reporters there was no way the first family could live within the $6,000
annual mansion operating budget.

The Turners never considered the governor's mansion their home.
They spent much of their time at their ranch, and both the governor
and first lady believed the mansion was a public place and that privacy
for its occupants was almost impossible.

After the legislature adjourned in late spring, the Turners moved
their base of operation to the ranch, often staying at the mansion only a
few nights each month. When they spent weekends in Oklahoma City,
the Turners were active members of the Crown Heights United
Methodist Church.

The most memorable Christmas in the mansion for the Turners was
their last. In December, 1950, a few days before Christmas, Turner
picked up a $31 million check to finance the Turner Turnpike between
Oklahoma City and Tulsa, the climax to a four-year battle with the
legislature and bond underwriters.

Governor Roy Turner's
prowess as a songwriter
was heralded in the
October 2, 1949 issue of
The American Weekly.
Courtesy The Oklahoma
Historical Society.

The Governor Decided to Deliver the
Goods. It Came the Hard Way, One
Note After Another as the Melody
Took Shape in His Mind.

Song Writing
Governor

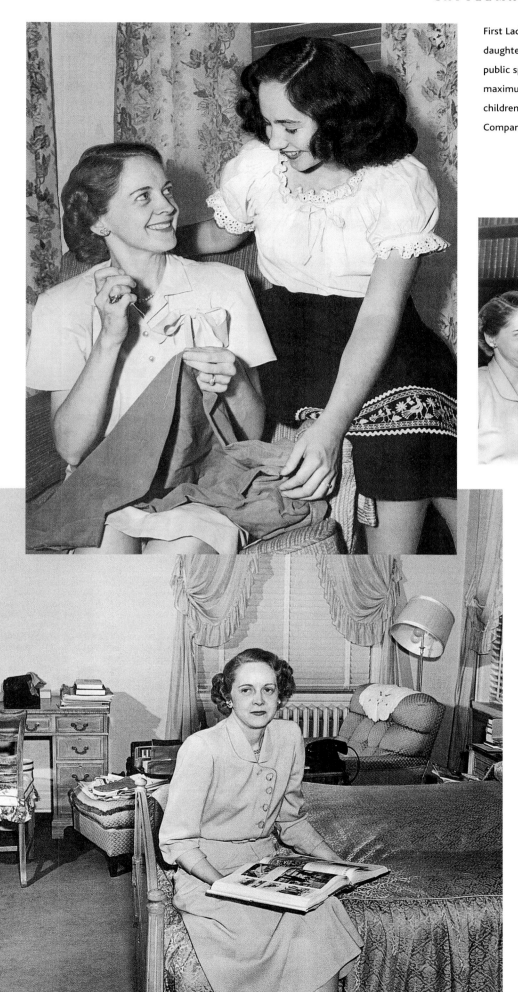

First Lady Jessica Turner, left, sewing with her daughter, Betty. Mrs. Turner did not cherish the public spotlight and planned her days for maximum participation in the lives of her children. Courtesy Oklahoma Publishing Company.

First Lady Jessica Turner, left, and Oklahoma Adjutant General W.S. Key, right, watch while Oklahoman and New York Yankee baseball great Allie Reynolds seals an envelope containing the official time for the 1950 *Oklahoma City Times* Christmas baby. The three were judges in the annual contest that awarded a prize to the baby born in Oklahoma City on Christmas Day nearest to the time written and sealed in the envelope. Courtesy Oklahoma Publishing Company.

The first lady relaxes with a book in one of the mansion's bedrooms in March, 1949. Mrs. Turner was an avid reader. Courtesy Oklahoma Publishing Company.

Even with professional movers to do most of the work, First Lady Jessica Turner still had to do much of the sorting for the move from the mansion. Courtesy Oklahoma Publishing Company.

First Lady Jessica Turner takes one last look from a mansion window toward the State Capitol as the Turners moved from the mansion in January, 1951. Courtesy Oklahoma Publishing Company.

Friends brought quail to the mansion for an all-family quail breakfast on Christmas morning. It was the only Christmas that all members of the Turners' immediate family were together on Christmas Day.

No one ever wanted to be governor of Oklahoma any more than Turner. He was a progressive Democrat who recognized the highly bureaucratic nature of state government and tried to maximize its efficiency through consolidation of state agencies, increased funding for common schools, and the creation of a better transportation network. He helped farmers cope with the demands of mechanization and supported new facilities for mental patients, prisoners, and abandoned children. He was inducted into the Oklahoma Hall of Fame in 1957.

After they left the governor's mansion, the Turners maintained a suite in the Skirvin Tower Hotel in Oklahoma City. He served many years as a member of the Oklahoma Highway Commission. He and the former first lady busied themselves in farming and the cattle business. They sold the Hereford Heaven Ranch to Winthrop Rockefeller in 1963 but continued to operate a 2,800-acre ranch along the Arkansas River in LeFlore County.

Turner worked to bring the National Cowboy Hall of Fame and Western Heritage Center to Oklahoma City and was involved in Oklahoma's early television industry. A brain tumor took his life in Oklahoma City on June 11, 1973. Mrs. Turner was a member of Crown Heights United Methodist Church in Oklahoma City and was active in the American Legion Auxiliary, the Oklahoma Cowbelles, and the National Hereford Association. She died at age 66 on March 2, 1981.

For further information on the Roy J. Turner family, see:

Stewart, Roy P. *The Turner Ranch: Master Breeder of the Hereford Line* (Oklahoma City: Homestead House, 1961)

Fischer, Leroy H. *Oklahoma's Governors 1929 to 1955 Depression to Prosperity* (Oklahoma City: Oklahoma Historical Society, 1983)

GOVERNOR JOHNSTON MURRAY AND FIRST LADY WILLIE MURRAY PROUDLY CALLED THEMSELVES "JUST PLAIN FOLKS" AS THEY MOVED INTO THE GOVERNOR'S MANSION IN JANUARY, 1951.

Governor and Mrs. Murray in the reception hall at the governor's mansion. The photograph was inscribed to Colonel Clive Murray, former state director of Selective Service and president of Murray State College from 1931 to 1961. Courtesy Kirk Rodden.

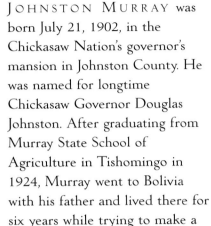

PLAIN FOLKS

JOHNSTON MURRAY was born July 21, 1902, in the Chickasaw Nation's governor's mansion in Johnston County. He was named for longtime Chickasaw Governor Douglas Johnston. After graduating from Murray State School of Agriculture in Tishomingo in 1924, Murray went to Bolivia with his father and lived there for six years while trying to make a success of his father's colonization expedition. He received his law degree in 1946 and was serving as the secretary of the Oklahoma School Land Commission when he announced his candidacy for governor in 1950.

First Lady Willie Emerson Murray, born in Weatherford, Oklahoma, in 1909, was Johnston Murray's second wife. They were married in 1933 after meeting at a Democratic state committee meeting a year earlier. The future Mrs. Murray was head of the piano department at Southwestern State College at Weatherford and served as vice chairman of the Custer County Democratic Party. As a musician she often appeared in public recitals and one season accompanied Metropolitan Opera Company soprano Martha Lipton.

Mrs. Murray played a major role in her husband's campaign for governor in 1950. She helped create the "just plain folks" theme and traveled to all corners of the state asking voters to elect her husband.

First Lady Willie Murray's open house at the governor's mansion each Thursday was so popular that often there were not enough hostesses to conduct tours. Greeted by this crowd of more than 1,200 visitors in April, 1953, cook, Ardis Wharry, houseboy, Thomas Jefferson Robinson, and guard, Walker Bozarth, were given hostess duties for the afternoon. More than 60,000 people visited the governor's mansion during the Johnston Murray administration. Courtesy Oklahoma Publishing Company.

After the mansion was renovated during the Johnston Murray administration, the music room was decorated in Pacific blue with a shrimp-colored upholstery for the sofa. Over the grand piano hung a Goetz portrait of the governor. Aqua sculptured carpet covered the entire first floor, the staircase, and the upstairs hall. Courtesy Oklahoma Publishing Company.

First Lady Willie Murray and Governor Murray have coffee in the newly decorated family dining room in October, 1951. The chartreuse and dark green room had been the guard's room in previous administrations. Chintz cottage curtains repeated the wallpaper pattern. Courtesy Oklahoma Publishing Company.

Governor Murray was sworn in by his father, former governor William H. "Alfalfa Bill" Murray. The aging legend said he was proud to do for his son what his father had done for him 20 years previously. Present at the inauguration were former governors Henry S. Johnston, William J. Holloway, Leon Phillips, and Roy J. Turner. Guards had to block off hallways in the State Capitol to control the thousands of citizens who attended a reception following the inauguration. The Murrays did not hold an inaugural ball.

Economy in government and no new taxes were the theme of the Murray administration. He urged the legislature to consolidate boards and commissions, eliminate unnecessary agencies, and equalize ad valorem taxes. Most of Murray's program was rejected by the legislature. Persuasive speeches, that struck a favorable chord with citizens, damaged his attempt to develop a good working relationship with legislators. However, Murray did cooperate with the legislature in the continuation of a highway improvement program.

Mrs. Murray was the first governor's wife to undertake a major redecoration and remodeling of the governor's mansion. Students from

The sunroom was on the south side of the mansion, opening off the state dining room. During the Murray administration it was strictly tropical from its hemp rug to the Philippine rattan furniture. The fragile-appearing draw drapes were actually narrow vertical strips of bamboo on the wall. The furniture was upholstered in a native flower print against a vivid red background. Throughout the mansion Mrs. Murray used a deep blue green shade of paint, commonly called "Willie Murray green." Courtesy Oklahoma Publishing Company.

First Lady Willie Murray was a fashion trend setter. She was a regular shopper at downtown Oklahoma City stores. She is shown here in a squaw dress, a style she adored because of her interest in Native American fashion. The dress became a fashion symbol in Oklahoma and was worn by women in elaborate velvets and taffetas for evening and more casual fabrics for daytime. Tour guides at the mansion adopted the squaw dress as the official uniform.

Oklahoma A & M College in Stillwater completely modernized the mansion kitchen, installing new cabinets and stainless steel appliances.

The college students made the birch cabinet doors in the pantry and the grandfather clock in the hall. Prisoners at the state penitentiary at McAlester made the nylon parachute cord rug in front of the fireplace in the upstairs living room.

The first lady had a tiny kitchen, complete with a combination stove-refrigerator, installed in the brightly painted yellow upstairs living quarters closet. Mrs. Murray painted flowers on the top of tables, built by Governor Murray, in the music room.

The entire first floor, winding staircase, and upstairs hall of the mansion were covered with aqua sculptured carpet. The dining room chairs and two chairs in the library were covered in coral.

Outside the mansion, Mrs. Murray took a great interest in adding flower beds and shrubs to the mansion lawn. She convinced state officials to dig a water well to supply ample water for mansion plantings.

In March, 1951, the first family opened the mansion to the public for the first time for weekly visits. Cookies and coffee, in cups stamped "Just Plain Folks," were served to more than 1,000 visitors. Mrs. Murray developed a detailed plan in which she determined the exact number of volunteers necessary to staff the open house properly, including a sentry at the top of the stairs to prevent visitors from hitting their heads on the low ceiling.

The open house was so successful that Mrs. Murray opened the mansion every Thursday from 2:00 p.m. to 5:00 p.m. She told a reporter that she got the idea on inauguration day when she saw thousands of people waiting hours to shake her husband's hand. The first lady said, "Some day I want to welcome them at the mansion." It is estimated that more than 60,000 Oklahomans toured the governor's mansion during the Murray administration. The crowds caused state officials to finally pave Phillips Avenue just west of the mansion. The street had been nothing but dirt and gravel for a quarter century.

Life Magazine covered Mrs. Murray's second open house that drew 2,246 visitors. On the Murray's 19th wedding anniversary in 1952, open house attendance hit a record 3,212. That week the Atchison, Topeka, and Santa Fe Railroad ran a special train from Kansas, bringing Kansans to tour the Oklahoma executive mansion. Mrs. Murray developed an impressive list of hostesses for the mansion open houses. Wives of legislators and other state officials and leaders from women's farm and home organizations helped serve coffee and doughnuts to visitors. The hostesses were dressed in festive dresses called "squaw dresses" at the time. The first lady stood at the door with a clicker in her hand to record the number of visitors.

Mrs. Murray invited Oklahoma artists to display their paintings in the mansion. The tall red-haired first lady loved the arts and tried to do her part to promote Oklahoma artisans.

The mansion kitchen was a variety of sparkling chrome, polished metals, and wood. The kitchen was well used during open houses at the mansion. Often 2,000 cookies were baked for the weekly event. Courtesy Oklahoma Publishing Company.

First Lady Willie Murray talks with workers outside the gate of the governor's mansion during the paving of Phillips Avenue west of the mansion grounds. The paving project was necessary because of large numbers of visitors to the mansion. Courtesy Oklahoma Publishing Company.

She opened her home to many civic groups that wanted to use the facility for dinners. She hosted 1,000 teachers during a meeting of the Oklahoma Education Association and gave numerous teas for home demonstration clubs and county Democratic women's groups. The silver service used to host groups was a gift to the Murrays from the Mexican government.

Although Johnston and Willie Murray were childless, Johnston Murray, Jr., his son by a first marriage, and Governor Murray's father, the legendary "Alfalfa Bill," lived at the mansion with the first couple for much of the administration.

Willie Murray was a popular first lady. She shook thousands of hands and appeared before civic and charitable groups. She developed a "traveling medicine show" of Oklahoma products and used them to decorate the mansion. The Oklahoma products were displayed in the mansion ballroom.

Mrs. Murray unsuccessfully tried to succeed her husband as governor in the 1954 Democratic primary because at that time an Oklahoma governor could not succeed himself. One of her biggest supporters was her father-in-law, "Alfalfa Bill." Mrs. Murray finished seventh in a field of sixteen candidates, receiving 20,000 votes.

The Murrays were involved in a sensational and bitter divorce case after they left the governor's mansion. When she died of cancer April 4, 1963, at the age of 54, *The Daily Oklahoman* called her Oklahoma's "most popular first lady." It has been said she never got over the failure of her 22-year marriage to Murray.

A month before her death the Oklahoma State Senate passed a resolution praising her for her contributions to promote Oklahoma and Oklahoma products. The resolution said, "Possessed with beauty, charm and wit, with a vigorous and independent personality, with the imagination of the artist, and with the talents of the virtuoso, she has ever scanned the horizons for new and consuming challenges."

Governor Henry Bellmon granted one of Mrs. Murray's last wishes, to lie in state on the second floor rotunda of the State Capitol. She was one of only two first ladies ever afforded the honor. The other was her mother-in-law, former first lady Alice Murray.

Typical of Mrs. Murray's personality was her request that an autopsy be performed on her body following her death, with "hope that these findings might benefit others."

As governor, Murray improved the state's turnpike system and inaugurated a program to build state lodges. After his term as governor ended, Murray moved to Fort Worth, Texas, where Oklahoma State Senator Gene Stipe found him driving a taxi. Stipe gave the former governor a job in his law office in Oklahoma City. Murray was later a staff lawyer for the Oklahoma Department of Public Welfare. He died April 16, 1974.

For more information on the Johnston Murray family, see:

Fischer, LeRoy H., editor. *Oklahoma's Governors 1929 to 1955 Depression to Prosperity* (Oklahoma City: Oklahoma Historical Society, 1983)

Former Governor "Alfalfa Bill" Murray, left, sometimes lived in the governor's mansion with son Johnston and First Lady Willie Murray. The elder Murray had sworn in his son as governor in January, 1951. Here the first lady prepares to leave the mansion in a helicopter. She was the first Oklahoma gubernatorial candidate to campaign in a helicopter. Courtesy Oklahoma Publishing Company.

Raymond Gary was a strong governor who used his experience in the State Senate to work well with the legislature. Courtesy Oklahoma Historical Society.

CHILDHOOD SWEET HEARTS

GARY RODE A HORSE to school from his family farm six miles outside Madill. He was born between Kingston and Madill January 21, 1908. Mrs. Gary, born October 2, 1907, at Kingston, was valedictorian of her high school class and was the only girl Gary ever courted.

The future first lady made her home, her family, and her church a priority as her husband attended Southeastern State College. The difficult Depression years made it hard to support his family, so Gary did not complete his college requirements. However, he was awarded a teacher's certificate and became a public school teacher. He was elected Marshall County School Superintendent in 1934, at the age of 26. At the time, he was the youngest person to ever hold that position in Oklahoma.

Mrs. Gary worked alongside her husband when he entered the oil business and politics. Gary was state senator from Marshall County from 1941 until he became governor in 1955. In the Senate, he was recognized as an expert on state finance and served as chairman of the powerful Appropriations Committee.

When Governor Gary was inaugurated in January, 1955, he chose not to have a formal inaugural ball. However, he and the new first lady greeted friends and supporters at a reception following the inauguration. Several hundred Marshall County supporters came en masse to Oklahoma City and hosted a dinner at the Oklahoma Club that evening.

As first lady, Mrs. Gary concentrated on improving the beauty of the grounds surrounding the governor's mansion. Her personal project was the rose garden on the west side of the mansion. Later the rose garden was named the Emma Gary Rose Garden.

Mrs. Gary oversaw a major re-landscaping of the mansion grounds. Overgrown plants were trimmed. Newer ornamental shrubs were added to produce blooms and berries for all seasons. More than 1,000 new shrubs and thousands of bedding plants were added to the mansion under the direction of Dr. Robert Rucker, landscape architect at the University of Oklahoma.

Governor Raymond Gary and First Lady Emma Gary entertain their grandchildren, left to right, Dan Gary, Emily Waymire, and Andy Waymire, in the music room of the governor's mansion. Courtesy Mona Gary Waymire.

First Lady Emma Gary, an award-winning gardener, supervised the construction of the Emma Gary Rose Garden on the west side of the governor's mansion. Courtesy Oklahoma Publishing Company.

The Gary children served Christmas dinner for employees of the Sooner Oil Company in 1955. Left to right, Jerdy Gary, Anne Hamill Gary, Mona Gary Waymire, and Dale Waymire. Courtesy Mona Gary Waymire.

The marker commemorating the renovation of the mansion grounds during the administration of Raymond Gary has since disappeared. Robert Rucker, landscape architect at the University of Oklahoma, developed the landscape plan. Courtesy Oklahoma Publishing Company.

Curving border gardens followed the fence that surrounded the mansion. Forsythia, crepe myrtle, Russian olive, red leaf plum, and redbud trees were planted to provide year round color and variety. Hundreds of perennials were added to the gardens. Possibly the most visible change in the landscaping was the addition of evergreen junipers to separate the mansion from the kennel, vegetable garden, and maintenance shed.

Inside the mansion Mrs. Gary used many pieces of her personal furniture to decorate the second floor of the mansion. The Garys' strong Baptist tradition was exemplified in the mansion reception room where a Bible and a rose graced a table.

By the time the Garys moved into the mansion, only son Raymond Jerdy, a junior at the University of Oklahoma, remained at home. Their daughter, Mona Mae, had married Dale Waymire. Soon Jerdy married Anne Hamill. Both of the Gary children quickly produced grandchildren to be entertained in the governor's mansion by the governor and first lady. A baby bed became a useful new piece of mansion furniture during the Gary administration.

The Garys considered themselves to be common Oklahoma people. When son Jerdy and wife Anne had their first baby at Fort Sill, base officials and Gary supporters spent a great deal of time and effort decorating the main gate for the arrival of governor and Mrs. Gary. However, the Garys slipped in a back gate and avoided the commotion.

Governor Gary's rural roots affected the mansion fare. Staples at most lunches and dinners, in season, were raw onions and fresh tomatoes. Gary always requested toothpicks following the meal.

Faithful daily Bible readers, Governor and Mrs. Gary were dedicated Baptists who lived what they preached. Courtesy Oklahoma Publishing Company.

Trustees from the state penitentiary in McAlester lived in the apartment over the mansion garage and provided cleaning, washing, and cooking chores for the first family. The first Christmas in the mansion was a big one for the Gary family. They invited employees from Governor Gary's Sooner Oil Company in Madill to eat Christmas dinner at the mansion. About 40 employees chartered a bus to make the trip. After a turkey dinner, served by members of the first family, the employees were taken by the governor on a tour of the Capitol and Oklahoma City.

The mansion library during the Gary administration. The leaded glass doors had been removed from the library bookshelves. Courtesy Oklahoma Publishing Company.

The Garys spent only two Christmases at the mansion. The governor and first lady were extremely family oriented and preferred spending holidays with their families at Madill.

Mrs. Gary enjoyed hosting teas at the mansion to raise money for worthy causes. She also oversaw functions in connection with Oklahoma's semi-centennial celebration and the opening of the Indian Exposition in Lawton.

After four years in the mansion Raymond and Emma Mae Gary returned to their Marshall County home and lived out their lives. Mrs. Gary was active in the Kingston Baptist Church and taught a junior girl Sunday School class for 15 years. She was a charter member of the Madill Rose Garden Club and was active in her home demonstration club, in the state Federation of Women's Clubs, and the Marshall Memorial Hospital Pink Ladies Auxiliary.

Mrs. Gary's devotion to her husband and family was best said by a friend, "She reminds me somewhat of Bess Truman—whatever their husband wanted, they were with them and doing their best."

In 1977 the Garys gave a gift of land and money to the Baptist General Convention of Oklahoma for the founding of a children's

The mansion music room. Note Governor Raymond Gary's portrait on the wall. Courtesy Oklahoma Publishing Company.

The upstairs living room during the Gary administration was simply decorated with flowered curtains and a solid color sofa. Courtesy Oklahoma Publishing Company.

A unique view of the state dining room and the mansion library during the Gary administration. Courtesy Oklahoma Publishing Company.

home just south of the Gary home between Madill and Kingston. The first cottage was named the Emma Gary Cottage.

The Garys had been married 63 years when she died in 1992. Governor Gary, remembered as one of the state's most powerful governors, probably is best known for his skillful handling of school desegregation in Oklahoma in 1955. He considered the Oklahoma Better Schools Amendment to the state constitution, industrial promotion, and road and highway development as the primary accomplishments of his term. Nearly 4,000 miles of new and resurfaced highways were completed under Gary's leadership. The Oklahoma Commerce and Industry Department was established as the spokesman for Oklahoma's growth and *Oklahoma Today* Magazine was launched during the Gary administration as the state's official magazine. Gary died December 11, 1993, at the age of 85.

For more information on the Raymond Gary family, see:

Milligan, James and L. David Norris. *The Man on the Second Floor: Raymond Gary* (Muskogee: Western Heritage Books, 1988)

Top: Governor Raymond Gary's study on the second floor of the mansion. Courtesy Oklahoma Publishing Company.

Inset: Governor and Mrs. Gary receive a gift from a visitor to the mansion. Courtesy Oklahoma Publishing Company.

THE GOVERNOR'S MANSION WAS A LONELY PLACE IN JANUARY, 1959, AS JAMES HOWARD EDMONDSON, THE STATE'S YOUNGEST GOVERNOR, AT 33, WAS SWORN IN ON THE STEPS OF THE NEARBY STATE CAPITOL.

AN OKLAHOMA PRAIRIE FIRE

THE ONLY INDICATION OF LIFE at the mansion was a guard standing by the front entrance. Inside, the mansion showed signs of its age. The green carpeting on the first two floors was worn and faded by time, sunlight, and past footsteps of

Jeannette and J. Howard Edmondson were a team all their lives. They went to school together and enjoyed a happy time with their children in the governor's mansion. Courtesy Oklahoma Publishing Company

thousands of people. There were six different colors of carpet in the mansion's four bedrooms located on the second floor.

The few remaining furnishings from the days of the original occupants during the Johnston administration showed heavy use and age. In some areas paint had peeled and plaster had chipped. The heating equipment and plumbing fixtures were outdated. The mansion was simply not fit for occupancy by Oklahoma's first family.

Edmondson, born September 27, 1925, in Muskogee, was a handsome, dynamic, and dedicated public servant who moved to Tulsa after three years in the Air Force and graduation from the University of Oklahoma School of Law. He was elected Tulsa County Attorney twice before entering the gubernatorial race in 1958. Edmondson's "prairie fire" campaign swept him into the governor's office with the greatest majority of votes to that time.

In 1946, Edmondson married Jeannette Bartleson, from Muskogee, a girl he had known all his life. They were in the same Sunday School class at Muskogee's First Presbyterian Church. The future first lady attended Hollins College in Roanoke, Virginia, and graduated from the University of Oklahoma in 1946.

The *Ladies Home Journal* featured First Lady Jeannette Edmondson in a fashion article in October, 1959. The magazine said Mrs. Edmondson looked fashionable and attractive whether she was dusting chandeliers or pouring tea at an official state function. Courtesy *Ladies Home Journal*.

The governor's mansion was a lonely place during the 1959 renovation. Governor J. Howard Edmondson and his family lived in a two-story home in the Heritage Hills section of Oklahoma City during the renovation. Courtesy Oklahoma Publishing Company.

Actor Dale Robertson was honorary grand marshal of the Edmondson inaugural parade through downtown Oklahoma City as fighter planes from the Oklahoma Air National Guard flew over the festive scene. An elaborate inaugural ball, the first in Oklahoma in 20 years, was held at the State Fairgrounds Arena.

While Governor Edmondson and First Lady Jeannette decided the future of the mansion, the Edmondsons and their three grade-school age children lived in a rented two-story house in the Heritage Hills section of Oklahoma City at 400 Northwest 19th Street.

First Lady Jeannette Edmondson and Jimmy, 13, Patty, 8, and Jeanne, 11, prepare for the Edmondson's first Christmas at the mansion, 1959. Courtesy Oklahoma Publishing Company.

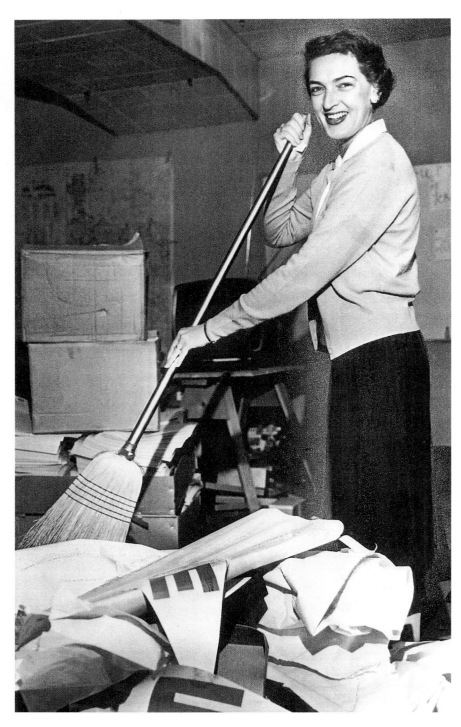

Right: First Lady Jeannette Edmondson led hundreds of volunteers in cleaning, painting, and renewing the inside of the governor's mansion in the spring and summer of 1959. They found battered, dirty furniture piled in the mansion's leaky basement. A newspaper reporter said the volunteers had given the mansion the prettiest "new look" in all its 31 years. Courtesy Oklahoma Publishing Company.

When the Oklahoma legislature convened in 1959, there was talk of either renovating the mansion or buying or building better quarters for the first family. House and Senate members converged on the mansion to inspect it. Representative John Levergood of Shawnee was an outspoken critic of those who suggested Oklahoma needed a new executive residence. Levergood said, "There's not a damn thing wrong with that mansion. That carpet on the floor is the same kind I've got in my house and I paid $18.75 a yard for it." Representative J.D. McCarty of Oklahoma City chided Governor Edmondson, saying "quite a few folks in Capitol Hill [the section of Oklahoma City McCarty represented] don't quite have anything like this." Another legislator suggested the mansion was certainly good enough for hay storage. Representative W.D. Bradley of Addington believed "with a little

Part of the 1959 mansion renovation was refurbishing the sunroom off the main dining room. The new heating and cooling system made the mansion more comfortable and eliminated unsightly radiators in each of the rooms. Courtesy Oklahoma Publishing Company.

Above: The breakfast room was an often-used nook in the mansion. First Lady Jeannette Edmondson often pitched in to help the mansion cook prepare meals for surprise guests. Courtesy Oklahoma Publishing Company.

Top left: The walnut paneling in the mansion library was bleached and rubbed to a warm glow during the Edmondson renovation. The fireplace was made into a working fireplace. For years its flue had been faulty. Courtesy Oklahoma Publishing Company.

Left: The music room was the most formal room of the renovated mansion. All the Edmondson children studied piano. Patty was the star; Jeanne did well; but Jimmy begged out of continuing lessons. Courtesy Oklahoma Publishing Company.

decoration and some minor repairs," the mansion could be made livable. Bradley said, "I know multi-millionaires who live in worse places."

Governor Edmondson, the nation's youngest governor at the time, believed that the mansion was not old enough to have tradition or historic value and that taxpayers would be best served by using the mansion for state offices and build new quarters for the first family.

In April, 1959, as legislators debated whether or not to renovate the mansion, First Lady Jeannette Edmondson spoke out on the subject. Even though some legislators who had toured the mansion had pronounced it "dandy for receiving company," the first lady listed the reasons why she believed the lawmakers should be embarrassed by what condition she found the mansion.

The new kitchen in the mansion was equipped with the latest in cabinets and appliances donated by Dulaney's. A new illuminated drop ceiling was added in the 1959 renovation. The first lady found the mansion to be like a small hotel. It had to be geared to produce practically anything at anytime. She was never sure how many were coming for dinner but Mrs. Edmondson was always prepared. An excellent cook, she helped in the kitchen and, in times of emergency, she was known to descend to the laundry and iron 11 shirts at what the housekeeper called "a lively clip." Courtesy Oklahoma Publishing Company.

Serving as a family den, the upstairs sitting room was modernized with sleek tables on which rested decorative lamps and a blue and terra cotta fruit bowl. New drapes and beige carpet were added in 1959. Courtesy *Living for Young Homemakers* Magazine.

The first lady found gas fumes swirling through the laundry room, high-water marks on the basement walls, shaky banisters on the great curving staircase, and water-soaked ceilings peeling upstairs. Also observed were great splits in the soiled, dark green drapes in the dining and reception rooms, old washing machines, "which have kept repairmen trotting to the site," and grease and dirt ground into every piece of overstuffed furniture. The leaky basement was full of old furniture.

The first lady defended her decision not to move immediately into the mansion. She said the home was fine for her family but was not suitable as an official residence. The days of piece-meal repairs and using inmate labor as household help had taken its toll.

Lawmakers continued their running battle in the press with Governor Edmondson. Senator Ed Berrong of Weatherford, a real estate agent when he was not serving in the legislature, found the mansion to be well built and suggested a healthy appropriation to finance repairs. State Senator Ray Fine of Gore, Edmondson's sharpest critic, charged that the public had been led to believe that the mansion was a run-down shack.

Eventually, the governor and first lady announced their plan for volunteers to plaster, paint, and repair the mansion. Edmondson used the legislature's failure to appropriate sufficient money to renovate the executive residence to his advantage. He said, "We felt the legislative problems of the people of Oklahoma were more important than the official residence of the state. So we decided to spend our energy in pushing for our reform program for schools, roads, welfare and general government instead of asking the legislature for an appropriation to make repairs on the governor's mansion."

"Where's my scrub pail?" asked Jean Abney, one of the Edmondson volunteers who brought her own ladder in case it was needed. She was part of the small army of workers who entered the mansion in early May, 1959. Every inch of the three-story house was scrubbed, and paneling was bleached and rubbed to a golden glow, a move that historical preservationists frowned upon in later years.

Sorey, Hill, and Sorey, architects, sent three mechanical and electrical engineers to the mansion. A.J. Bullard Decorators donated consultation on interior decoration. The Allied Paint Company gave dozens of gallons of paint to restore the interior. Dulaney's Manufacturers and Distributors donated new kitchen equipment.

Perched on a carton full of books in the library, the first lady asked, "What's the best way to clean books?" Sixteen volunteers, all veterans of Edmondson's prairie fire campaign the previous year, joined state maintenance workers in tearing out old cabinets and repairing ceilings. Old, rusting radiators were replaced with a modern air conditioning and heating system. The third floor ballroom was junked as such and was turned into a huge playroom for the three Edmondson children, Jimmy, age 11; Jeanne, age 9; and Patty, age 7.

The Edmondsons changed the appearance of the outside of the governor's mansion by removing heavy ivy planted in the Marland administration that covered many of the walls.

In mid-July, the first family moved into the renovated mansion. The first lady estimated that volunteer labor along with donated materials, appliances, and heating and cooling equipment had saved taxpayers $65,000. Mrs. Edmondson had used $4,000 in state money and $1,500 she borrowed personally to be repaid from the $1,250-a-month mansion operating allowance. She replaced gaping shelves and cupboards and bought sheets, towels, and bedroom curtains. She also squeezed money to purchase lamps, tables, kitchen pots and pans, and a gleaming electric crystal chandelier for the state dining room.

"The second floor is where we 'lived,' " Jeanne Edmondson recalled. "Our bedrooms, Mom's office, and family room were there. The family room housed our television and came complete with a built-in refrigerator for pop and goodies."

"The main floor of the mansion was where the action was," Jeanne said. "My parents loved to entertain and most every night there were extra people for supper and visiting in the living room. We kids were included in most every occasion. Our most memorable evenings were when movie stars came to the house. Danny Kaye made a special point

First Lady Jeannette Edmondson, in the white sweater, shows the mansion dining room to Shirley Bellmon, right, and Bellmon daughters, left to right, Pat, Gail, and Ann, after the December, 1962 election. Courtesy Oklahoma Publishing Company.

of going up to visit my sister when she was in bed with the measles. John F. Kennedy, Robert Kennedy, and J.D. McCarty were visitors in our home. J. D. even rode my brother's go-cart around the front lawn of the house."

On October 15, 1959, Mrs. Edmondson hosted an open house to honor the volunteers who had made the mansion renovation possible. The first lady took all the crticism over the renovation project in stride, saying, "I've simply done what Oklahoma women have been doing ever since the pioneer days—I've made a home for my husband and children."

Living for Young Homemakers Magazine featured the mansion and Mrs. Edmondson's restoration project.

Edmondson's term as governor was marked by progressive measures that sparked controversy, possibly the most politically unsettling term in state history. He fulfilled his pledge to defeat the hypocrisy of prohibition. His reform programs, including reduction of patronage in state jobs and the creation of central purchasing, challenged the foundations of Oklahoma government. As a result, the days of rural legislators and the Democratic Party dominating Oklahoma government were numbered. The youthful governor moved a politically reluctant Oklahoma into its modern era.

Edmondson resigned as governor after Robert S. Kerr died January 1, 1963, and was appointed to replace Kerr in the United States Senate. However, he lost his bid for re-election in 1964. He retired to private law practice in Oklahoma City and died suddenly of a heart attack, at age 46, November 17, 1971.

Jeannette Edmondson outlived her husband by almost two decades. She later married E.E. Duffner, an Oklahoma City builder, and obtained her real estate brokerage license. She was appointed by Governor George Nigh as Oklahoma Secretary of State in 1979.

A surprise visitor to the swearing in ceremony was daughter Jeanne Edmondson Watkins who flew to Oklahoma City from her home in Mobile, Alabama, without advance warning. The Edmondson family numbers had dwindled with the death of Governor Edmondson in 1971 and son James H. Edmondson, Jr., in 1976. Mrs. Edmondson served as Secretary of State for eight years and was elected president of the National Association of Secretaries of State and was a board member of the American Heart Association. She died July 11, 1990.

Twin beds permitted a steady stream of small overnight guests in the three Edmondson children's bedrooms. This is Jeanne's domain, all cotton-candy pink. Courtesy Oklahoma Publishing Company.

For more on the J. Howard Edmondson family, see:

Fischer, LeRoy H., editor. *Oklahoma's Governors 1955-1979 Growth and Reform*

(Oklahoma City: Oklahoma Historical Society, 1985)

"RELAXED AND SMILING, GEORGE NIGH ARRIVED SUNDAY AT THE PLACE HE AIMED FOR LAST MAY AND MISSED—THE GOVERNOR'S OFFICE," BEGAN REPORTER KATHERINE HATCH'S FRONT-PAGE STORY IN *THE DAILY OKLAHOMAN* ON MONDAY MORNING, JANUARY 7, 1963, UNDER A HEADLINE, "BIG JOB IS NIGH'S IF ONLY FOR WEEK."

George Nigh was a bachelor when he served his first term as Governor in January, 1963. State newspapers called him Oklahoma's most eligible bachelor. Courtesy Oklahoma Publishing Company.

NINE DAYS OF NIGH

GEORGE PATTERSON NIGH, age 35, a native of McAlester, veteran of the Oklahoma House of Representatives, and the state's youngest Lieutenant Governor ever, had lain awake the night before, planning his next few days as chief executive. He had become Governor in possibly Oklahoma's most exciting two weeks of political history.

Senator Robert S. Kerr died January 1, 1963, allowing Governor J. Howard Edmondson to resign and be appointed to Kerr's United States Senate seat by Governor Nigh.

With his parents and his three brothers and sister in attendance, Supreme Court Justice Earl Welch formally swore in Nigh as the 17th Governor of Oklahoma at 10 a.m. on Monday, January 7, 1963. The brief ceremony was witnessed by an overflow crowd of family and friends in the Blue Room of the Capitol, just feet away from the cavernous office occupied by Oklahoma's chief executive. Nigh and United States Senator Edmondson received a rousing ovation from the throng.

In a brief statement after he took the oath of office, Nigh called on the people of Oklahoma to double their efforts to carry the state forward. Reflecting on the death of Senator Kerr, Nigh said, "It is with regret that I even have the opportunity to serve you as governor."

Nigh talked with friends and family on the telephone constantly, inviting them to Oklahoma City to stay in the mansion or to become members of his staff, a time called by Martin Hauan, "nine turbulent

Governor Nigh's parents and his brothers and sister and their families were invited to the mansion during his brief 1963 term. This photograph was taken in the Governor's office at the State Capitol immediately before Nigh was sworn in as Governor. Courtesy Oklahoma Publishing Company.

Governor Nigh invited his nieces and nephews to a first-class slumber party at the governor's mansion during his nine-day term in 1963. Courtesy Oklahoma Publishing Company.

Thousands stood outside the mansion waiting their turn to shake Governor George Nigh's hand during the open house in January, 1963. Visitors braved sub-freezing temperatures for the honor. Courtesy Oklahoma Publishing Company.

days filled with cots and happiness...stately rooms filled with cots and roll-aways. The mansion's long, winding 3-stories banister...a thrilling roller coaster for dozens of squealing kids."

The new Governor invited his nieces and nephews, uncles, aunts, cousins, and some of their friends for a sleepover at the mansion. Still a bachelor, Nigh closed his Lieutenant Governor's office and moved his secretary, Glenda Temple, to the Governor's office. He appointed Paul Carris as chief of staff, Joe Johnson as legal counsel, and other friends and supporters as aides to the Governor. The Biltmore Hotel provided cots and roll-away beds for friends and relatives to sleep on at the mansion. As was the custom, the outgoing Governor had removed much of the bedroom furniture from the mansion so even Nigh, the Governor, had to sleep on a roll-away bed.

With only one cook officially remaining on duty, Nigh and his new staff ate three meals a day at the mansion. The first affair was a state dinner, complete with candles, china, and historic silverware on the big dining room table. However, the cook had gone home for the day, so pizza was ordered in for the occasion.

Nigh announced a gala event to close out his nine-day administration, an open house at the governor's mansion, on Sunday from 1:00 to 5:00 p.m., complete with cookies and punch. He appointed 12 Oklahoma City women to an arrangements committee. Wynetka Armor was chairman with Dolly Hoskins, Glenda Phillips, Mrs. David Bridges, Mrs. John Ingram, Mrs. Lewis Darrell, Crystal Mounts, Mrs. John Perry, Mrs. Cruce Trice, Billie Fagerquist, Mrs. John Conners, and Mrs. Ben Brown as committee members. Another 50 women were named to a reception and tour committee.

Nigh's close advisers told him that the size of the crowd at the Sunday open house at the mansion would be a referendum on his drive to push through approval of the Lake Eufaula lodges. He had fired the entire State Planning and Resources Board and appointed new members who would approve a contract with the federal government to build the Arrowhead and Fountainhead lodges on Lake Eufaula. If only a handful of people showed up, his advisers reasoned, Nigh's actions would be deemed a failure. Conversely, if a large crowd attended the event, it would be a sure sign of approval of his leadership.

The morning dawned with teeth-chattering cold gripping the state all the way from Boise City to Broken Bow. It was three degrees below zero at 8:00 a.m. as volunteer committees began arriving at the mansion with punch bowls and cookies. Nigh feared the bone-chilling temperatures would severely limit the crowd.

He had invited everyone, and it seemed as if they all came. Thousands showed up before the gates opened. Nigh saw people huddled in the cold on both sides of Northeast 23rd Street and gave the order to open the gates early. Planners had expected only a few hundred people, but literally thousands swarmed over the mansion grounds, "looking at books, studying the kitchen, climbing the spiral staircase" and finally meeting their host, the Governor.

Mrs. Howard Everest, one of the official greeters, estimated that 20,000 to 22,000 people visited the mansion that was so clogged with visitors that the fire marshal halted the serving of refreshments. Cars were parked for blocks around.

The official guest book was signed by 10,000 people. The signing started out at the front door, but as the crowd grew, the book was split three ways. There was a logjam at the few bathrooms in the mansion. People waited up to a half hour outside bathroom doors.

Nigh worked the crowd, shook hands with everyone, and kissed more than a few babies. Doing what came naturally, he stayed until the last Oklahoman left the open house. He loosened his tie and sat down with friends on the historic staircase inside the mansion's front entrance. He was pleased with his fellow citizens' response to his invitation to the open house. All agreed that it sent a signal that indeed Nigh was still a major player in Oklahoma politics. It was a fitting end to the first term of Governor George P. Nigh.

For more information on George Nigh, see:

Burke, Bob. *Good Guys Wear White Hats: The Life of George Nigh* (Oklahoma City: Oklahoma Heritage Association, 2000)

Fischer, LeRoy H., editor. *Oklahoma's Governors 1955-1979 Growth and Reform* (Oklahoma City: Oklahoma Historical Society, 1985)

A CHANGE OF POLITICS

Henry Bellmon proposed to Shirley Lee Osborn on their third date. They were married six weeks later, January 24, 1947. Bellmon served in the United States Marines in World War II, winning the Silver Star for service on Saipan and the Legion of Merit in action on Iwo Jima. Courtesy Henry and Shirley Bellmon.

BELLMON, born near Tonkawa, Oklahoma, September 3, 1921, was a true grassroots politician. He bought the suit he wore for high school graduation with money he had raised selling skunk and opossum hides. Bellmon graduated from Oklahoma A & M College in Stillwater with a degree in agronomy in 1942. He served in the Marines in World War II. His combat duty on Iwo Jima earned him the Silver Star and Legion of Merit. The Silver Star was earned for valor while carrying a wounded crewman to safety through withering gunfire after a molten armor-piercing shell killed the tank's gunner, who died where he sat between Bellmon's legs.

Returning from the war to the family farm near Billings, Bellmon met and married a neighbor girl, Shirley Osborn, in January, 1947. He had been elected to the Oklahoma House of Representatives the year before.

Shirley Osborn, born in Billings on August 5, 1927, was the first member of the family to get involved in politics. She was a GOP state committeeman from Noble County in 1954. By 1960 Henry and Shirley Bellmon

Left: Shirley Bellmon, an accomplished seamstress, often made identical dresses for her stairstep daughters. Left to right, Pat, Gail, and Ann. This was the 1958 Bellmon Christmas photograph. Courtesy Henry and Shirley Bellmon.

Below: The new Governor, Henry Bellmon, and First Lady Shirley Bellmon dance after the grand march at the January, 1963 inauguration. Courtesy Oklahoma Publishing Company.

were the parents of three active daughters, Pat, Gail, and Ann. Bellmon was the State Republican Chairman and was the obvious choice as the party's nominee in the 1962 gubernatorial campaign.

Campaigning was a family affair with the girls joining their parents that summer traveling around the state. A series of "two-party" teas and Main Street campaign stops by the family created a grassroots victory that would be duplicated in subsequent Bellmon campaigns.

Capitol veterans did not know how to take Bellmon. He often went to work at 2:30 A.M., drove his own car, used old envelopes to write inter-office memos, and went about his job as governor in an unheralded way. It was suggested that Bellmon was not as colorful as past chiefs such as "Alfalfa Bill" Murray or Robert S. Kerr. Reporter Wilbur Martin wrote, "Bellmon isn't a tobacco-chewer fighting abominable oil baron, a spell binding stump orator or a hell-raising reformer. He simply goes about his business the same way he's always done it."

Bellmon won the hearts of many Oklahomans with his humble attitude, complete honesty, excitement about economic development, and promises of no new taxes.

The governor's mansion in 1963. Courtesy Oklahoma Publishing Company.

More than 20,000 Oklahomans jammed the State Capitol for an informal inaugural ball in January, 1963, to greet their new Governor and first lady. Governor Bellmon refused to wear a tuxedo but Mrs. Bellmon personally created for herself a simple, light beige, wool suit with a tiny fur collar for the inauguration and a short evening dress and matching coat for the inaugural ball. The dress and coat were made of blue brocade. The dress had side-draped pockets trimmed in tiny pearls. The first lady wore blue shoes, a pearl necklace, and an orchid corsage to the ball. The beige suit won third place at the State Fair of Oklahoma the following September.

As Governor, Bellmon had to deal with the controversial issues of legislative reapportionment and the deteriorating condition of the state's public schools. He strongly believed that state government should improve schools and other programs without tax increases. His conservative, unwavering stand on the tax issue often put him at odds with leaders of the legislature. However, Bellmon was able to push funding for five new state turnpikes through the legislative process.

The governor's mansion was a world apart from the Bellmon's sprawling Billings ranch home. The Bellmon daughters were allowed to select a favorite color for their bedrooms. The three-room apartment over the mansion garage was repainted and served as living quarters for Katherine Christie, the first lady's social secretary.

The Bellmons brought to the governor's mansion the same standards they had set for their personal lives and entertaining. No alcohol was served in the mansion during their administration. Citizens from across Oklahoma were invited to see the mansion in a series of Sunday afternoon receptions. Dinners were held to allow the Governor to get acquainted with members of the legislature and the Capitol press corps. The Bellmon daughters often served guests at the formal and informal dinners. Mrs. Bellmon's pecan pie was a household favorite.

The first lady, an accomplished seamstress, took her sewing machine to the mansion. She and her daughters created much of their own clothing. Mrs. Bellmon prepared breakfast and lunch for her family. The mansion cook helped the first lady when large groups gathered for meals at the executive residence.

First Lady Shirley Bellmon swaps recipes with Chef Frank Stockwell, a member of the American Culinary Association, in preparation for a Food-A-Rama, in which Mrs. Bellmon participated. She was an experienced cook having prepared meals for farmhands on the Bellmon's Billings ranch. She cooked for luncheons and dinners at the mansion. Spaghetti was her specialty for guest functions. She was an avid gardener and canned many fruits and vegetables from the Bellmon farm. Canned apple butter and fresh peach preserves lined the mansion pantry shelves. Mrs. Bellmon once baked 25 pecan pies for a series of mansion dinners. Courtesy Oklahoma Publishing Company.

The first lady kept her sewing machine busy during her time in the governor's mansion. She enrolled in a pattern-making course at Central State College in Edmond. The remodeled family breakfast room was Mrs. Bellmon's sewing headquarters for personal and fair sewing projects. The first lady used pecan paneling to cover murals that had been papered on the walls of the breakfast room in the Edmondson administration. Courtesy Oklahoma Publishing Company.

Modeling an all-cotton shirtdress and white coat during a style show for wives of members of the Oklahoma Livestock Marketing Association is First Lady Shirley Bellmon in February, 1963. Courtesy Oklahoma Publishing Company.

First Lady Shirley Bellmon puts the finishing touches to a rose peau de soie dress she created for a Republican Party rally in late February, 1964, in Oklahoma City. During her time in the governor's mansion, Mrs. Bellmon also made time to work a replica of the state seal into end tables with ceramics and gave one as a gift to each of the governor's 16 staff members one Christmas. Courtesy Oklahoma Publishing Company.

Mrs. Bellmon bought a bed and borrowed a chest from the Oklahoma Historical Society for the master bedroom. The Bellmons brought their own grand piano to the mansion but left most of their furniture at the Billings farm where the family spent a great deal of time.

Moving three teenage girls from Billings to Oklahoma City proved to be quite an adventure. They attended Wilson Elementary School and Classen Junior and Senior High schools. However, they adjusted well, even though youngest daughter Ann fractured her arm at Wilson.

The first lady set aside three days per week strictly for family. She catered to the needs of her husband and daughters. Unless affairs of state interrupted, dinner was a family affair at the mansion. The Bellmons talked politics and family. Mrs. Bellmon believed political discussions were educational for her daughters.

Life at the mansion is remembered by the Bellmons as simply fun. It was home first and then an official residence. Slumber parties, family Christmases, birthdays, and other holidays were mixed comfortably with official functions. Ann talked a Capitol policeman into letting her sit on the lions atop the State Capitol. Polly, the mansion cook, made the best chocolate chip cookies in the state, or so thought the Bellmon girls. Gail Bellmon Wynne recalled, "Our time in the mansion was a time of creating memories with an understanding of the responsibility that few have the good fortune to enjoy."

Even though they lived in the governor's mansion in Oklahoma City, Mrs. Bellmon and her daughters still participated in the Noble County Fair in 1963. The first lady won first place for her sewing in the tailored garment division. Gail placed first with her corn meal muffins and Ann won the blue ribbon for her mosaic painting. All three Bellmon girls had several seconds, thirds, and fourth place entries at the county fair.

The Bellmon daughters were active in 4-H Club and were assisted by their mother in seamstress projects. The first lady installed a cutting table on the first floor of the mansion and enrolled in a clothing design course at Central State College in Edmond.

The first lady accomplished her goal of putting her family first in the governor's mansion. A newspaper feature article said, "If the state's first lady has trouble finding time to squeeze in sewing, her daughters certainly haven't picked up any extra time since moving into the mansion. Gail is likely to be taking an accordion lesson while Pat is getting ready for a piano lesson while Ann is packing her slippers for a ballet lesson."

All three daughters took piano and voice lessons. Pat played the saxophone and twirled for the Classen High School Band in Oklahoma City. Gail played the clarinet in the band.

The Bellmons continued their tradition of down-home hospitality, especially for their extended family. Once they entertained 75 family members at one dinner.

In 1965, efforts were renewed to build a new governor's mansion. Representative Percy Butler of Tulsa, calling the mansion "bleak and desolate looking," asked the Legislative Council to study the feasibility of constructing a new half-million dollar mansion on state property near the State Capitol. Governor Bellmon appointed a special committee to look into the suggestion. The committee was chaired by Representative William Skeith of McAlester. Other members were State Senator G.O. Williams of Woodward; Charles Duffy of Ponca City; Mrs. Frank Davies of Enid; Charles E. Clew, Jr., of Ardmore; Turner Stallings of Oklahoma City; and Mrs. Beachy Musselman of Shawnee.

Skeith's committee sought advice from former Oklahoma first ladies and sent a questionnaire to governor's wives in all states that had built new mansions within the past 15 years.

Oklahoma newspapers supported building a new governor's mansion. Inadequacies of the mansion were described as lack of privacy for the Governor and his family, lack of outdoor recreational activities such as a pool or barbecue area, lack of entertaining space, and lack of a separate building to house mansion guards. The first lady often stepped over guards who were performing their duties in the home of the first family. One guard slept at night on a cot in the mansion entryway.

After studying governor's mansions in 29 other states and reviewing an engineering report from the Oklahoma Board of Affairs, the Skeith committee recommended building a new governor's mansion and turning the old mansion into a museum. The committee voted unanimously in favor of the plan and asked for a public donation of land. The well-based suggestions of the Skeith committee were ignored by legislative leaders and plans to build a new Oklahoma governor's mansion were scrapped.

After leaving the governor's mansion, Bellmon was national campaign manager for Republican presidential nominee Richard Nixon. Bellmon was elected to the United States Senate in 1968 and served until he chose not to run for re-election in 1980. After serving as Director of the Oklahoma Department of Human Services for a short time in the George Nigh administration, Bellmon was elected Governor of Oklahoma a second time in 1986.

For more information on the Henry Bellmon family, see:

Bellmon, Henry with Pat Bellmon. *The Life and Times of Henry Bellmon* (Tulsa: Council Oaks Books, 1992)

The Bellmon family leaves the mansion at the end of their four-year term in office. They were recreating the same scene in the mansion that "Alfalfa Bill" Murray and his wife Alice posed for when they left office in 1935. Courtesy Oklahoma Publishing Company.

Campaign insiders described Ann Bartlett as the "sense of humor" for the couple. A campaign aide said, "When Dewey got to taking himself too seriously, boy, she'd bring him back to earth." Courtesy Oklahoma Publishing Company.

Facing page, top: First Lady Ann Bartlett and her children, left to right, Mike, Joanie, and Dewey, Jr. Courtesy Ann Bartlett Burke.

Facing page, inset: First Lady Ann Bartlett was active in many civic and charitable organizations. One of her favorites was a group that raised money for missionary work and the construction of a hospital in Guatemala. Mrs. Bartlett made a trip to Guatemala to observe work of the organization. Courtesy Oklahoma Publishing Company.

DEWEY FOLLETT BARTLETT AND FIRST LADY ANN SMITH BARTLETT MET AT A USO DANCE AT LAGUNA BEACH, CALIFORNIA, DURING WORLD WAR II.

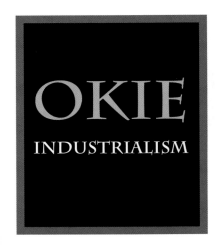

OKIE
INDUSTRIALISM

YOUNG BARTLETT, born in Marietta, Ohio, March 28, 1919, graduated from Princeton University and received flight training at the Naval Air School in Norman, Oklahoma, on his way to leading numerous raids on Japanese targets in the South Pacific as a Marine dive bomber pilot. He received the Air Medal for his exploits.

It was love at first sight. Ann Smith was reared in Seattle, Washington, but was visiting her grandmother in southern California when she met her future husband at the dance. After a whirlwind courtship, they fell in love. When Bartlett returned from his 18-month tour of duty, they were married on April 2, 1945, in California's historic San Juan Capistrano mission.

Bartlett was born to be an oilman. His father and grandfather had been active in early oil exploration. He had come west to Oklahoma in the summers of 1940 and 1941 to work in the Oklahoma oil fields around Dewey, Bartlesville, and Konawa. He returned with his family in 1946 and settled in Tulsa where he built a successful independent oil business, Keener Oil Company.

Mrs. Bartlett was director and secretary for the Tulsa Family and Children's Service agency while raising her young children.

While recovering from hepatitis in 1960, Bartlett began reading books on politics and volunteered to serve on a committee in 1962 to draft an opponent for the Democratic state senator in Tulsa County. When the committee could not find a candidate, Bartlett decided to run himself. Asking his daughter, Joanie, what she thought about it, she said, "Go for it Daddy." Bartlett warned his young daughter that he might lose but Joanie replied, "Well tough bazookies." Bartlett was elected as a Republican senator from Tulsa County on the same day that Henry Bellmon became the first Republican Governor of Oklahoma.

On November 8, 1966, the eve of Ann Bartlett's 46th birthday, her husband was elected Governor. Bartlett was the first Catholic to contend seriously for the Oklahoma Governor's office. *The Washington Post* called Bartlett's victory "the end of political religious bigotry in Oklahoma."

Six former Oklahoma Governors, George Nigh, J. Howard Edmondson, Johnston Murray, Raymond Gary, William Holloway, and Henry Bellmon, looked on as Bartlett was inaugurated January 9, 1967. An inaugural dinner was held in the Imperial Ballroom at the Skirvin Hotel in Oklahoma City. Special wine glasses with the state emblem were at each place on round tables in the dining room. During the dinner, film clips and slides from previous inaugurations were shown. After a rousing standing ovation, the new Governor and first lady traveled in a special police motorcade to the State Fairgrounds Arena where thousands more were waiting to cheer them. Mrs. Bartlett wore a hyacinth pink chiffon gown with a flowing back panel and in her hair was a jeweled pink velvet bandeau.

As Governor, Bartlett promoted Oklahoma with a highly successful "Okie" pin program. He used the name given Oklahomans heading west in John Steinbeck's *Grapes of Wrath* as a positive slogan for proud Oklahomans. Bartlett heavily promoted the development of the state's natural resources and improved vocational technical education and mental health facilities. He also appointed Oklahoma's first black district judge, Charles Owens, of Oklahoma City.

When the Bartletts moved into the mansion, two of their three children were already in college. Dewey, Jr., 19, returned to Regis College in Denver, Colorado. Joanie, 18, was a freshman at Colorado State University. Mike, 17, had already enrolled at Oklahoma City's Casady High School after the Christmas break and was staying with friends until the remainder of the first family moved from Tulsa.

Above: The punch bowl from the battleship USS *Oklahoma* is used to serve punch at a reception for state legislators at the governor's mansion in January, 1967. Courtesy Oklahoma Publishing Company

Right: The First Lady and Governor Bartlett prepare to welcome guests during the Christmas season at the mansion. Courtesy Oklahoma Publishing Company.

The new first lady stood by her husband's side for three hours in a grueling reception line following the inauguration. She looked fresh and relaxed in a two-piece camel hair suit, a mink hat, and alligator shoes. The suit and hat were new, but the shoes had been a gift from her husband many years before.

Even though liquor had been legalized in Oklahoma during the Edmondson administration, the Bartletts jointly decided to not serve liquor at public or official state gatherings, including functions at the mansion.

Ann Bartlett was a gracious and practical first lady. One of the first problems she faced in her new home was how to eliminate static electricity generated when she shook visitors' hands in the mansion. Someone suggested purchasing a $100 humidifier. Instead, Mrs. Bartlett bought $6 worth of spray for the carpet which drastically reduced the shocking static electricity.

The Bartletts moved only one piece of furniture, a spinet piano, into the mansion from their Tulsa home during their first months in the mansion. She later added furnishings to an upstairs sitting room and moved their own dining room furniture into the sunroom. This move increased seating to 24 persons for dinners.

The first lady turned the third floor ballroom, which had not been used for that purpose in many years, into a recreation room for Mike and his friends. Mike occasionally used the room to practice his electric guitar. However, the ballroom was occasionally placed into use as an overflow dining room when downstairs dining facilities would not accommodate large crowds. Waiters carried food and drink from the kitchen all the way to the third floor.

The first lady found the 39-year-old mansion "usable and workable." She recognized that a larger first family might have problems fitting into the structure and was concerned with the absence of a large room for dinner parties and receptions. She oversaw the repainting of two of the upstairs bedrooms. Because he did not want any appearance that he and his family might benefit personally, Governor Bartlett asked the legislature to delay any action on proposals to build a new governor's mansion.

The only structural change in the mansion during the first year of the Bartlett administration was the construction of cabinets to hide the radiators under the windows in the sunroom.

The first lady placed paintings and sculptures by Oklahoma artisans throughout the mansion. The most notable sculpture was a buffalo by Joe Taylor of the University of Oklahoma. The first lady wanted the

First Lady Ann Bartlett and Governor Dewey Bartlett showed their support for children's issues by hosting day care students at the mansion. Courtesy Ann Bartlett Burke.

buffalo in the sunroom, but the Governor insisted it be placed on a pedestal at the foot of the mansion's spiral staircase.

Mrs. Bartlett did much of the cooking for the first family. However, she was assisted by a cook three days a week, a housekeeper five days a week, and a laundress one day a week. Wilhelmina Cooper was a terrific cook who loved to show off her talent by baking all types of pies, cookies, and cakes. Her turkey, chicken, ham, and beef entrees were popular with visitors to the mansion. Wilhelmina wanted to please the Bartletts. If one of the children said, "strawberry is my favorite," a strawberry delicacy was likely to appear at the next meal.

Above: The quiet Ann Bartlett approached the legendary Henry Wade at the first floor information booth at the State Capitol in January, 1967, after her husband was sworn in as governor. Wade, not recognizing the first lady, approached Mrs. Bartlett and asked if he could show her around the Capitol. Wade said, "Lady, where are you from?" He was embarrassed when the kind first lady informed him she was gathering information for a program on the Capitol. Courtesy Oklahoma Publishing Company.

Right: First Lady Ann Bartlett was chairman of the Indian Crafts booth at the Oklahoma City Festival of the Arts in 1970. To practice properly handling the handmade crafts, Mrs. Bartlett wears a Cherokee shawl and Cheyenne-Arapahoe necklace. Courtesy Oklahoma Publishing Company.

While breakfast was being prepared, Governor Bartlett was often jogging around the mansion side yard. He determined how many laps around the perimeter made up a mile. For a change of pace the Governor simply changed directions of his morning jog.

Once while preparing for an early morning meeting of university and college presidents, Mrs. Bartlett climbed the stairs to the third floor to check on arrangements, not realizing that it was time for the guests to arrive. The educators were polite and did not comment on the first lady's curlers and slippers.

The Bartletts spent their first Christmas in the mansion as they always had, with family and plenty of good food. Only the location was different for Christmas 1967. A wreath made of pine cones decorated the front door of the mansion just as it had added a cheerful holiday note to the Bartlett home in Tulsa for many years. Bartlett's brother, David, joined the Governor, first lady, and the three children for Christmas dinner. The Bartletts attended midnight mass at nearby Corpus Christi Catholic Church.

The mansion music room became Governor Bartlett's study and office. The first lady moved a walnut dining table, buffet server, and silver cabinets into the mansion from the governor's late mother's home in Marietta, Ohio.

A "Friends of the Governor's House" committee was formed to assist Mrs. Bartlett in locating pieces of historically significant furniture for the mansion. A four-man committee oversaw purchases.

The first lady, who had a greenhouse at her Tulsa home, actively planned spring plantings each year she lived in the mansion. She started plants in boxes in the basement and on the mansion sun porch. The kitchen became a miniature greenhouse. She brought thousands of flower seeds from her Tulsa collection but delegated the actual planting of periwinkles and Shasta Daisies in the large flowerbeds that surrounded the mansion.

The Okie pin became the emblem of the Bartlett administration. The gold pin featured a rain drop and pine tree. Bartlett passed them out by the thousands and at one time the pin was a semi-official part of the uniform of Oklahoma Highway Patrol troopers. Courtesy Oklahoma Publishing Company.

The mansion library was simply a room with a bunch of shelves and very few books. A Bartlett friend, John Bennett Shaw, president of the Oklahoma Library Association (OLA), suggested to the first lady that the mansion library be stocked with quality writings. At Mrs. Bartlett's request, the OLA and Oklahoma Department of Libraries provided hundreds of books to fill the empty shelves. The mansion library was finally a real library with books for children as well as adults and several reference books used by the Governor while working at home. The new library gave Dewey Bartlett, Jr., a keen interest in the history of World War II and the Civil War.

The first lady set out to make the mansion historically significant. She began collecting a memento, a picture, piece of furniture, anything, from each of the previous Oklahoma Governors. Her first acquisition was a framed 1906 white admission card to a banquet honoring territorial Governor T.B. Ferguson. University of Oklahoma President George L. Cross sent the first lady a copy of Governor Charles N. Haskell's certificate of election.

The memento collection grew. A copy of a $31 million check, which paid for the Turner Turnpike, recalled the days of Governor Roy J. Turner. Governor Bellmon donated a wooden elephant. Mike McCarville gave an old photograph of Governor Lee Cruce driving a golden spike in the Oklahoma, New Mexico, and Pacific Railway at Ardmore in 1913. Other mementos included Governor Leon Phillips' pipe and belt, Territorial Governor Martin Trapp's ashtray, Governor Henry Johnston's gavel, a dozen dessert plates owned by first lady Amy Holloway, and an engraved silver platter from Governor Charles Haskell.

In November, 1968, the Bartletts unveiled the painting *Oklahoma Wheat Harvest*, by Peter Hurd. The painting, commissioned by Secretary of Commerce C.R. Smith, formerly of Tulsa, was painted by Hurd as a gift in trust of Governor and Mrs. Bartlett to hang permanently in the governor's home. Mrs. Bartlett was also interested in day care center development, improvement of state libraries, and enjoyed knitting.

In 1970, debate over the issue of constructing a new governor's mansion surfaced again. State Insurance Commissioner Joe B. Hunt said the mansion "looked like a jailhouse" and that a new mansion should be built to allow a Governor space to entertain and meet with his department heads. Hunt, known for his colorful language, said, "Maybe the legislature could make a museum out of it and call it the 'Okie Alamo' because of the many political battles that have been fought there."

Pressed on the matter, Governor Bartlett refused to support the building of a new mansion, instead calling for a legislative appropriation to build an addition to provide a reception room and dining facilities for large groups. Again, the thought of any major changes in the mansion fell on deaf ears at the legislature.

When son Mike graduated from high school and entered college at

The snow-covered mansion grounds in February, 1968. Courtesy Fred Marvel.

Princeton University, the first lady had more time for membership on boards and committees of several organizations. She was active in the League of Women Voters, the Collectors Group of Philbrook Museum, the Mission Board for Guatemala, and the Oklahoma Association for Retarded Children.

In 1972, two years after his term as governor ended, Bartlett was elected to the United States Senate where he served until lung cancer forced him to decide not to seek re-election in 1978. He died March 1, 1979, a few weeks before his 60th birthday. Mrs. Bartlett was later married to John Burke, a college professor, who also died of lung cancer. She was active in the work of the Tulsa chapter of the American Cancer Society.

For more information on the Bartlett family, see:

Burke, Bob and Kenny Franks. *Dewey Bartlett: The Bartlett Legacy* (Edmond: University of Central Oklahoma Press, 1996)

David Hall was elected Governor in 1970 in a stunning upset over incumbent Governor Dewey Bartlett. His charismatic approach to campaigning won him widespread support. Courtesy Oklahoma Historical Society.

Late summer flowers line the mansion driveway in August, 1973. Courtesy Fred Marvel.

WHILE ATTENDING NIGHT CLASSES AT THE UNIVERSITY OF TULSA LAW SCHOOL IN DECEMBER, 1955, DAVID HALL MET AN ATTRACTIVE AMERICAN AIRLINES STEWARDESS, JO EVANS, ON A BLIND DATE. THEY WERE MARRIED SIX MONTHS LATER IN JUNE, 1956.

HALL OF OKLAHOMA FOR ALL OF OKLAHOMA

J O, a native of Morrilton, Arkansas, had lived in Tulsa just two days when she met her future husband. She had moved to Tulsa after completing college and stewardess training. After the Halls were married, Jo transferred to a ground job at American Airlines while Hall completed law school. Hall, born in Oklahoma City October 20, 1930, graduated from Classen High School where he was president of the student body. He was Phi Beta Kappa at the University of Oklahoma, making the list of top ten students in his junior and senior years. He waited tables in his fraternity house, sold hamburgers in dormitories, and was a clerk at a Norman clothing store to finance his education.

Jo Hall tries on a satin faille coat and dress that she wore at her husband's inaugural ball in January, 1971. The dress was made by Jennie Spagna of Oklahoma City, formerly a designer for Christion Dior of New York City. Courtesy Oklahoma Publishing Company

First Lady Jo Hall admires a silver plate owned by Governor Charles Haskell, part of the mansion collection of mementos from Oklahoma's first families. Courtesy Oklahoma Publishing Company.

Hall served as County Attorney of Tulsa County from 1962 until he unsuccessfully ran for the Democratic nomination for Governor in 1966. As County Attorney, he prosecuted more than 1,000 criminal cases with a 94 percent conviction record.

After four years of private law practice, Hall was the first candidate to announce for Governor in 1970. Using the campaign slogan, "Hall of Oklahoma for All of Oklahoma," Hall pulled off one of the state's greatest upsets by defeating incumbent Republican Governor Dewey Bartlett in the November, 1970, general election. Hall won the Governor's race by a razor-thin margin of 2,181 votes, the closest gubernatorial race in state history.

Hall was inaugurated on a windy 50-degree January day in 1971. The inaugural ball was held at Shepherd Mall, a large enclosed shopping center in northwest Oklahoma City. House Speaker Carl Albert of McAlester was the highest national official ever to attend an Oklahoma gubernatorial inauguration.

Above: The first family, December, 1973. Left to right, Doug, 16, First Lady Jo Hall, Governor David Hall, Nancy, 17, and Julie, 13. Hilda, the Hall's St. Bernard, was an integral part of the official family portrait. Courtesy Fred Marvel.

Right: First Lady Jo Hall, left, and Governor David Hall, right, hosted Governor and Mrs. James Exxon of Nebraska for Thanksgiving dinner at the mansion in November, 1971. The dinner preceded the Oklahoma-Nebraska football game, called by sports writers "the game of the century." Courtesy Oklahoma Publishing Company.

Hall's tax reforms put Oklahoma back on a sound financial basis at a time when the need for new state revenue had reached a crisis. His concern for education resulted in major efforts to raise per pupil state expenditures and hike teachers' salaries to the regional average. Hall also pushed legislation to decrease the state's high teacher-pupil ratio in public schools and proposed making kindergarten available and mandatory for all Oklahoma youngsters.

First Lady Jo Hall moved her family into the governor's mansion after the inauguration. The hustle and bustle of the mansion was far different than Mrs. Hall's childhood days on Rose Creek in rural Arkansas. She grew up in a remote community of only six families where the rare passing of an automobile was a celebrated occasion.

Mrs. Hall continued First Lady Ann Bartlett's tradition of collecting mementos of previous Governors and their families. She asked Mrs. Tom Birbiles and Mrs. Bill Nash, both of Tulsa, to organize a committee to make permanent historical acquisitions. Among items donated to the mansion collection through the efforts of the first lady and the committee was a hall tree that had belonged to Governor Henry Johnston. The piece had been used in Johnston's law office and was donated by his former secretary.

The new first lady staunchly defended the aging governor's mansion. She, as others before her, longed for more space to entertain large groups but believed the Oklahoma governor's mansion was better than many state-owned homes for chief executives in other states.

First Lady Jo Hall oversaw the renovation of the old fishpond on the grounds of the mansion in 1972. The pond was transformed into a beautiful reflecting pool. Courtesy Stuart Ostler.

First Lady Jo Hall, left, was joined by Mrs. Frank Loeffler, Jr., at an April, 1971, open house of the mansion for American Cancer Society volunteers. Courtesy Oklahoma Publishing Company.

The needlepoint cushion depicting the Oklahoma State Seal was part of the 1972 effort to recover chairs in the mansion dining room. The state seal was chosen for the host and hostess chairs. Courtesy Jim Argo.

Mrs. Hall brought a few pieces of furniture to the mansion from her home in Tulsa and added pewter candlesticks and old clocks to the mansion decorations. She and the housekeeper, Willie Mae Cook, pleasantly struggled with Governor Hall's constant promise of bringing two people to lunch or dinner and showing up with ten.

Admitting that she "cried every foot of the turnpike" from Tulsa to Oklahoma City when moving into the mansion, Mrs. Hall adapted to living under the constant scrutiny of the public and the press. She talked openly of cutting her long hair and buying a new wig, certainly a fashion statement in the early 1970s. She missed her friends in Tulsa but had little time to mourn her move to the mansion because of the heavy responsibility of caring for the Hall's three children, Julie, Doug, and Nancy.

With a new Governor in office, talk of a new governor's mansion was renewed in 1971. Governor Hall was opposed to the construction of a new mansion, even though some legislators and Board of Affairs members wondered how long the out-dated mansion could serve as a quality official residence for Oklahoma's first family.

President Richard Nixon planned to stop by the governor's mansion in November, 1971, on his way to the Oklahoma-Nebraska football game in Norman. The planned visit cost taxpayers $25,000 for a hard-surface helicopter pad behind the mansion, even though state officials had been considering building a pad for use by the Governor anyway. The helicopter pad was later converted into a tennis court for use by the first family.

Mrs. Hall used prison labor to assist in renovating the mansion in late 1971. The third floor ballroom was painted white. A warming kitchen was installed in a closet in the ballroom. Another ballroom closet was converted into a powder room. A blue shag carpet turned the garden type room into a facility that would seat 80 people for dinner. Prisoners built round table tops that fastened securely to folding bridge tables. Brown folding chairs were purchased.

The new first lady furnished the sunroom with painted Victorian wicker furniture and potted plants. It was used as a family breakfast room for the children when the Governor had a working breakfast in the official dining room. The sunroom was also used for games and entertaining.

Visitors to the mansion in February, 1972, found the Halls settled into the second floor living quarters, "13-year-old Doug setting up his barbells and ant farm; Nancy, 14, begging her mother for more than three guests to a party; and Julie, 10, hoping to have friends of her own over."

Mrs. Hall added new wallpaper and shutters in the ancient bathroom with its three kinds of mismatched tile and funny fixtures. The official guest room was Doug's room, which he joyfully vacated to a sleeping bag when an overnight guest was invited to the mansion.

The first lady announced a statewide needlepoint project in 1972 to complete chair covers in the state dining room. The 12 covers contained seals of the Five Civilized Tribes, other Oklahoma Indian tribes, including the Osage Nation, and designs of the state flower, bird, and tree. It was an impressive list of Oklahoma women picked to make the chair covers. Mrs. W.P. Atkinson, Mrs. E.V. Huggins, Mrs. LeMoyne Hickman, Mrs. Jack Helton, Mrs. George Webber, Mrs. Henry Leforce, Mrs. Jim Gregory, Mrs. Dianne Hickman, Mrs. Bill Richerson, Mrs. H.O. McIntosh, Mrs. Hal Pierce, Mrs. C.S. McMurray, Mrs. Tom Steed, and Mrs. R.W. Hudson were chosen to participate in the historic project. Mrs. Jon Rowntree of Oklahoma City designed the covers. In the closing days of the Hall administration, Governor Hall signed an executive order transferring ownership of the chairs to the Oklahoma Historical Society.

After a 1972 report was highly critical of security at the governor's mansion, Governor Hall instituted several changes. Highway patrol cadets, rather than college students, were hired to guard the grounds. A two-man patrol of the mansion was maintained around the clock. Electrical gates were installed to limit access to the mansion. Better lighting was added to the property surrounding the executive residence. The Halls also placed their children in schools outside the mansion district.

In 1974 landscape architect Ron Manley supervised an overhaul of the landscaping around the governor's mansion. Over the years, different clubs and organizations had donated patches of flowers or shrubs, but the first lady believed a comprehensive plan was necessary to convert the seven acres into a garden of which Oklahomans could be proud.

On a shoestring budget, Mrs. Hall drew from the two greenhouses on mansion property and added dozens of redbud trees, the official state tree, and other shrubs and perennials. She renovated the reflecting pond and wished for more ivy on the mansion to serve as a nesting place for birds. The first lady liked birds. She had a mynah bird that whistled at most guests who visited the mansion.

Governor Hall was defeated in his bid for re-election in 1974. Nine days after he left office as governor, Hall was indicted by a federal grand jury on four charges of bribery and extortion in connection with an alleged plan to receive payment for influence over investment of state retirement funds. Although he claimed innocence, Hall was convicted of bribery in March, 1975. He served 18 months in a federal correctional institution in Arizona and then moved to California to engage in real estate and investments.

For information on the David Hall family, see:

Fischer, LeRoy H., editor. *Oklahoma's Governors 1955-1979 Growth and Reform*

(Oklahoma City: Oklahoma Historical Society, 1985).

The design from the Oklahoma state flag graced the cushion of one of the chairs in the mansion dining room. Courtesy Jim Argo.

BOREN'S PLATFORM INCLUDED REQUIRING
COMPETITIVE BIDDING FOR STATE BANK DEPOSITS
AND FOR PROFESSIONAL SERVICES, CORRECTIONS
REFORM, CAMPAIGN FINANCE DISCLOSURE LAWS,
AND OPEN MEETING AND PUBLIC VOTING BY ALL
STATE LEGISLATIVE COMMITTEES AND STATE
BOARDS AND COMMISSIONS.

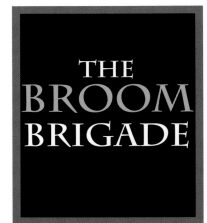

THE BROOM BRIGADE

Governor David Lyle Boren addresses thousands of friends and supporters on the south steps of the State Capitol on his inauguration day, January 13, 1975. The large crowd braved freezing temperatures. Courtesy David and Molly Boren.

DAVID LYLE BOREN was born April 21, 1941, in Washington, D.C., the son of former Oklahoma Congressman Lyle H. Boren and Christine Boren. David Boren graduated from Yale University; Oxford University, where he was a Rhodes Scholar; and from the University of Oklahoma School of Law.

Boren was elected governor of Oklahoma in 1974 with the help of a unique campaign symbol. Armed with brooms, the "Boren Broom Brigade" carried the young former legislator's pledge to "sweep out the Old Guard" and bring fundamental reforms to state government. A huge rally of more than 5,000 people carrying brooms was held on the steps of the State Capitol on the eve of the election.

Boren slipped past incumbent Governor David Hall into a Democratic runoff with favored Clem McSpadden. Boren beat McSpadden and swept past Republican challenger James M. Inhofe of Tulsa in the 1974 general election.

David L. Boren poses with a broom, sweeping off the state seal in the State Capitol. Oklahoma voters heeded Boren's call to "sweep out the Old Guard." Courtesy Oklahoma Publishing Company.

Reverend Robert Cooke, pastor of the First United Methodist Church of Seminole, performed the private wedding of Governor David L. Boren and Judge Molly Shi of Ada on November 27, 1977, at the governor's mansion. It was the first time in Oklahoma history that a governor was married while in office. Courtesy David and Molly Boren.

Dan Boren, right, celebrated his fifth birthday in August, 1978, at the governor's mansion. At left is his sister, Carrie, age seven. Courtesy Oklahoma Publishing Company.

Boren, at 33, was the nation's youngest governor when inaugurated on January 12, 1975. An outspoken supporter of the arts, Boren's inaugural activities carried a theme celebrating arts and culture in Oklahoma. An "Evening of the Arts" showcased the state's orchestras, dance companies, vocalists, and college ensembles. The new governor "glided smoothly from one performance hall to another" to simultaneous performances throughout the evening. An inaugural art exhibit featured Oklahoma's finest visual artists. Boren's talented family members livened the inaugural ball held at the Myriad Convention Center with musical entertainment by his cousin, popular singer Hoyt Axton and friend Arlo Guthrie, son of Oklahoman Woody Guthrie. Also in attendance was Boren's aunt, Mae Boren Axton, best know as the songwriter of Elvis Presley's first hit, *Heartbreak Hotel.*

As governor, Boren led the fight to reduce the Oklahoma inheritance tax. His age did not inhibit his leadership ability. As a highly educated person, Boren developed a distinct professionalism in his office. Through intelligence, compromise, and great resolve, his reform program enabled Oklahoma, a state ripe for government reorganization, to emerge with a more progressive and efficient structure. Boren led efforts for the first state funding of gifted and talented public school students, developed a

Left: First Lady Molly Shi Boren grew up at Stratford in Pontotoc County. After graduating from the University of Oklahoma School of Law, she practiced law before being appointed Special District Judge in Pontotoc County. Courtesy Oklahoma Publishing Company.

Above: First Lady Molly Boren, right, discusses plans for a governor's mansion reception with Mrs. Howard Smotherman, left, and Mrs. Johnny Jones, Jr. Courtesy Oklahoma Publishing Company.

leadership enrichment program, and established the Oklahoma Summer Arts Institute at Quartz Mountain State Park near Altus.

Shortly after graduating from law school in 1968, Boren married Janna Lou Little, the daughter of Oklahoma oilman and politician Reuel Little of Madill, who ran for governor as the candidate for the American Independent Party in 1970. The couple had two children, Dan and Carrie, before the marriage ended in divorce in 1975. The former first lady married a Texas oil producer, John Clinton Robbins, in 1976. She died in 1998 after a long battle with cancer.

First Lady Janna Boren placed strict limits on public use of the mansion in 1975. Citing the young ages of her children, Carrie, four, and Dan, two, Mrs. Boren allowed only statewide clubs, groups, or

THIS PROPERTY HAS BEEN
PLACED ON THE

NATIONAL REGISTER
OF HISTORIC PLACES

BY THE UNITED STATES
DEPARTMENT OF THE INTERIOR

A plaque was attached to the governor's mansion to certify its inclusion on the National Register of Historic Places. Courtesy Oklahoma Publishing Company.

organizations to use the mansion for social purposes. The Boren children were the youngest ever to live in the governor's mansion. Weekly public tours were eliminated although groups or clubs could schedule tours by reservation on the third Thursday of each month.

The Oklahoma legislature, recognizing the rising cost of maintaining the governor's mansion, raised the annual appropriation from $15,000 to $30,000 during the 1975 legislative session.

The mansion was the target of a Molotov cocktail incident in September, 1975. Two homemade explosive devices were placed outside the mansion gates but failed to explode. Security guards quickly extinguished the devices. The first family was unaware of the incident.

In 1976, the mansion was added to the National Register of Historic Places as part of the Capitol-Lincoln Terrace Historic District. Work had begun on the designation during the Hall administration.

In September, 1976, construction was completed on a new concrete block guardhouse at the east gate of the mansion. The new guardhouse was part of a security overhaul for the mansion. A modern closed-circuit television and lighting system complemented a new fire alarm and fire escape system implemented by the state Board of Public Affairs. John Coldiron, longtime mansion employee, directed guardhouse operations.

During the Boren administration, part of the mansion basement was again turned into a recreation room. The young Boren children spent much of their time in the new room.

Even though the mansion was no longer the permanent home of Boren's two children, it continued to express their presence. After the governor's divorce from Janna Boren, Dan and Carrie continued to spend almost all their time at the mansion. Nellie McDaniel, a member of the mansion staff, and her husband Lowell McDaniel, who worked for the Board of Public Affairs, lived in the mansion's garage apartment and assisted Governor Boren with the care of the children. The McDaniels, from Boren's hometown of Seminole, were longtime family friends. Carrie and Dan's grandparents, Lyle and Christine Boren, were also frequent visitors to the mansion.

The governor had a bicycle with two children's seats. He and his two children were often seen riding around the State Capitol complex on weekends. They often rode to pay Sunday afternoon visits to State Human Services Director Lloyd Rader, who allowed the children to take over his office while he and the governor talked business.

Carrie's room contained twin wooden beds covered with blue floral print bedspreads. In Dan's room was an antique brass bed that the governor had brought from his home in Seminole. Stuffed animals filled most corners and niches in the children's bedrooms.

Extraordinary security surrounded the marriage of Governor Boren to Pontotoc County Special District Judge Molly W. Shi on November 27, 1977. Only Boren's family and immediate top-level staff members knew of the approaching wedding until hours before the event. State required blood tests were sent to the laboratory under the names of John and Jane Doe. The governor avoided the public process of obtaining a marriage license from the district court clerk by utilizing a little-known state law that allowed a district judge to issue a marriage license. District Judge Ronald Jones of Ada issued the license and kept the secret until after the ceremony.

David and Molly Boren made history. It was the first time an Oklahoma governor was married while in office. They exchanged vows in the mansion with only immediate family members in attendance. The new first lady's wedding dress was a pale blue color and was made by her sister, Judy Connally.

First Lady Molly Boren was born in Ada, taught school after receiving an English degree from East Central State University, and completed her master's degree in English and law degree at the University of Oklahoma. She practiced law in Ada before being appointed Special District Judge in 1975.

Molly Shi and David Boren's first date was a memorable one. Boren's Chief of Staff Robert "Bob" Morgan, later Oklahoma's Adjutant General, had introduced them. After dinner at Oklahoma City's Gaslight Dinner Theater, they returned to the governor's mansion for coffee. Finding the coffee pot dry, the future first lady, decked out in a long evening gown, washed the coffee pot while the governor searched the mansion kitchen for cups and saucers. Being required to wash dishes on their first date was a source of kidding between the first lady and governor for years.

Molly Boren opened the governor's mansion to the public with a series of teas and receptions. Mansion staff members Doretha Hays and Marie Humphrey were kept busy making necessary arrangements. Hoping to share the mansion with as many people as possible, she targeted groups in rural areas, convincing clubs and groups from rural Oklahoma to make the governor's mansion a regular place of visitation.

One of the first lady's early events at the mansion was a private reception for her family and friends. Mrs. Boren especially enjoyed showing the mansion to some of the ladies she had grown up with from Stratford where she attended public schools.

Another early event was an open house for state employees at the Capitol complex and their families. It was held during the first Christmas season after David and Molly Boren were married. The reception, scheduled to last two hours, ended up being a day-long affair when more than 4,000 guests showed up to go through the receiving line.

Another large event occurred in 1978 when a reunion of the extended Boren family was held at the mansion. More than 200 family members attended. There was a family art exhibit featuring paintings by the governor's first cousin, James Boren, former art director at the National Cowboy Hall of Fame, and James Boren's daughter Nancy and brother Jodie.

The governor's aunt, Mae Boren Axton, presided over music performances by several Boren family members during the reunion at the mansion. Religious discussion and debates were led by uncles J.D. Boren and Dallas Boren, both Church of Christ ministers, and James Boren, a former Methodist minister and college president. As expected, politics was argued by everyone. The all-day event was described by Governor Boren as "a three ring circus" but at least everyone went home still on speaking terms.

Molly Boren had an excellent relationship with the Boren children, Dan and Carrie. The governor insisted his children not be spoiled by too much attention. He thought it important for the children to live a normal life.

The first lady gave the governor a blue Oriental lamp as a wedding present. However, the lamp ended up on the first lady's desk in the office at the head of the winding staircase on the mansion's second floor.

Mrs. Boren valued her privacy, grasping for moments she could

"First Kids" Dan and Carrie Boren listen to their father speak at a political rally during his successful 1978 bid for the United States Senate. Courtesy Oklahoma Publishing Company.

spend alone meditating, reflecting, and listening to American jazz. She loved music, especially works by Aaron Copeland. The first lady believed being alone was as essential to her well being as breathing and eating.

The first lady thought of herself as a country girl, a rural girl who married David Boren for the man he was, not because he was governor of Oklahoma. She supported the Equal Rights Amendment and believed that women should think for themselves and make their own decisions. She and the governor loved the out-of-doors and often hiked and spent weekends at a cabin at Beavers Bend State Park near Broken Bow in southeast Oklahoma.

One of the common threads of interest between the first lady and the governor was American Indian art. Not long after their marriage, the mansion was filled with sculptures, paintings, and prints by outstanding Oklahoma Native American artists.

During the Boren administration, bathrooms in the mansion were re-carpeted. Handyman Willie Schrantz, the official mansion maintenance man since 1959, oversaw the project. Schrantz had been hired to complete the renovation of the mansion during the Edmondson years. He stayed on for more than two decades and became irreplaceable because of his knowledge of the mansion's structure, its faults, and its attributes. Schrantz stayed lean and trim through his years in the mansion by carrying furniture, luggage, boxes, and equipment up and down the four floors of the executive residence.

Boren decided in January, 1978, to forego seeking re-election as governor. Instead he ran for, and was elected to, a seat in the United States Senate. Boren quickly was recognized as a national leader in the Senate where he served as chairman of the Senate Intelligence Committee. He resigned in 1994 to become president of the University of Oklahoma. Molly Boren became the first woman in Oklahoma history to serve as a trial judge, first lady of the State of Oklahoma, and first lady of the University of Oklahoma. Boren became the first Oklahoman to serve as a state legislator, governor, United States senator, and university president.

Mrs. Boren has been active in civic and charitable work, serving on the boards of banks, corporations, the Sarkeys Foundation, and the Oklahoma Arts Institute. Boren's interest in education is exemplified by his establishment of the Oklahoma Foundation for Excellence.

For more information on the David L. Boren family, see:

Burke, Bob. *Lyle Boren: Eloquent Congressman* (Edmond: University of Central Oklahoma Press, 1992)

Fischer, LeRoy H., editor. *Oklahoma's Governors 1955 to 1979 Growth and Reform* (Oklahoma City: Oklahoma Historical Society, 1985)

Above: George Nigh served as governor of Oklahoma longer than anyone else in history. Courtesy Oklahoma Publishing Company.

Right: Governor George Nigh and First Lady Donna Nigh. Nigh began his service to Oklahoma in 1950 when he was elected to the Oklahoma House of Representatives from Pittsburg County. Courtesy Oklahoma Publishing Company.

AFTER GEORGE NIGH SERVED NINE DAYS AS GOVERNOR IN 1963, HE LEFT PUBLIC OFFICE AND OPENED A PUBLIC RELATIONS FIRM.

GOOD GUYS WEAR WHITE HATS

NEWSPAPERS CALLED NIGH the most eligible bachelor in the state. He had dated but never found a girl he wanted to marry; that is, until he was introduced to brown-haired Trans World Airlines (TWA) ticket agent Donna Mashburn.

Even though the public thought of Nigh as a highly eligible bachelor, Donna wanted to know what the big deal was. The truth was that Nigh had no job, no house, no car, was a defeated candidate, and up to his ears

in campaign debt. However, his relationship with Donna blossomed. Nigh said it was love at first sight, but Donna was not sure. She was unaccustomed to appearing in public with a face that everyone knew.

The future first lady was a 30-year-old single parent with a 10-year-old son, Berry Michael "Mike" Mashburn, born October 8, 1952, during a previous marriage. Donna had graduated from Oklahoma City's Capitol Hill High School and attended Central State College in Edmond.

Many of the couple's dates were to the nearby University Hospital where Nigh's mother was hospitalized. Irene Nigh had lost a kidney and was receiving dialysis daily at the hospital.

It was difficult to find a romantic moment during the courtship because Nigh had no money for elaborate dates and Mike was usually along. However, in September 1963, Nigh planned a special way to ask Donna to marry him. Their favorite song was *I Left my Heart in San Francisco,* by Tony Bennett. One evening Nigh quickly pulled a record from an album cover and placed it on the turntable on Donna's stereo. His plan was to ask the magic question while Bennett sang.

Unfortunately, Nigh picked up a Judy Garland record about San Francisco. Instead of the melodic sounds of Tony Bennett, out came the raspy rendition of Judy Garland. But Nigh popped the question anyway.

Donna did not give Nigh an immediate answer. She had a lot to think about. She had proven she could take care of herself and Mike. She had a good job, a home, and an automobile. She knew she loved Nigh but wanted to make certain she was ready for marriage. After a week, maybe the longest in Nigh's life, Donna said yes. They were married October 19, 1963, at the Capitol Hill Baptist Church in Oklahoma City.

On January 14, 1965, Mrs. Nigh gave birth to Georgeann Nigh, a seven-pound, thirteen ounce girl for the Nigh household. Mike was 12-

First Lady Donna Nigh oversaw the first family's move from the mansion in the summer of 1979. The Nighs moved back into their Picnic Lane home in far west Oklahoma City while $98,000 worth of legislatively authorized renovations were completed on the mansion. The most costly part of the work was rewiring the structure and replacing windows with insulated glass. Courtesy Oklahoma Publishing Company.

Five first ladies of Oklahoma met at the governor's mansion in May, 1984, to honor the mansion's volunteer tour guides. Left to right, Shirley Bellmon, Donna Nigh, Ann Bartlett, Molly Boren, and Jeanette Edmondson. Courtesy Oklahoma Publishing Company.

years-old when Georgeann was born and was very proud of his new little sister. Soon he became a reliable babysitter.

In 1966, Nigh was again elected Lieutenant Governor of Oklahoma. In the 1978 gubernatorial race, he realized his life-long dream of being elected governor of Oklahoma, winning with a campaign theme of "Good Guys Wear White Hats." Governor Boren left office five days early to assume his new role as United States Senator. Boren resigned as governor at one minute before midnight on January 2, 1979. Constitutionally, Nigh, at that moment, became governor. However, he was not sworn in until January 3.

Nigh decided to hold his swearing-in ceremony outside Oklahoma City, the first time a governor had ever been sworn in outside the state capital of either Guthrie or Oklahoma City. He did not want to detract from his planned inauguration on the State Capitol steps five days later. Nigh chose Bartlett Park in downtown Tulsa as the site for his swearing-in. He wanted to emphasize that Oklahoma had two major metropolitan areas.

When Nigh was later sworn in for his full four-year term, it was actually the third time he had served as governor.

Nigh delivered his inaugural address at the State Capitol, not from a prepared text, but from strategic cryptic notes on his left hand. He had for most of his adult life written key words on his hand to refresh his memory when he stood before audiences. While waiting to be escorted onto the inaugural platform on the south steps of the Capitol, Nigh

peeled off his black leather glove to reveal yet another set of notes for
his inaugural speech.

The governor and first lady danced the night away during the
inaugural ball at the Oklahoma City Myriad Convention Center. Floyd
"Red" Rice's band was one of three musical groups who performed for
supporters who paid $5 each to attend the event. Mrs. Nigh wore a
dark blue, full-length dress. The top of the dress was covered in dark
blue sequins. The flowing skirt of sheer chiffon was belted at the waist.

While Nigh was working on his relationship with the diverse
membership of the Oklahoma legislature, Mrs. Nigh was settling down
in a new home, the 51-year-old governor's mansion.

The mansion needed rewiring, new carpet, energy efficient windows,
and sandblasting of the Indiana limestone exterior. Mrs. Nigh always
liked to point out that the mansion and Governor Nigh were born the
same year and that she "had to have the mansion sandblasted."

Life in the mansion for the Nighs was far different from life in their
Picnic Lane home by Lake Overholser in west Oklahoma City. Mike
had graduated from college and moved away. Guards and a high fence
prevented drop-in guests.

First Lady Donna Nigh decorated the mansion
in fall harvest colors in November, 1984.
Courtesy Oklahoma Publishing Company.

Mrs. Nigh decorated the mansion to
her taste, with the help of new personal
furniture and antique chairs and tables she
rescued from State Capitol storage rooms.
Then she invited the people of Oklahoma
to visit. Going against advice to open the
mansion for public visits, Mrs. Nigh
instituted a weekly open house;
Wednesday afternoons from 1:00 p.m. to
4:00 p.m. Hostess-guides were volunteers,
primarily from Democratic Women's
Clubs across the state. Mary Newsome
coordinated the weekly open house.

Mrs. Nigh was excited about opening
her three-story home to the public, saying,
"The mansion belongs to the people of
Oklahoma. We want to make sure it's
accessible to the public." The word
"accessible" also meant adding a ramp on
the back porch of the mansion to enable
people in wheelchairs to visit the mansion.
During the first open house after the
ramp was installed, a visitor noticed it and
said, "Oh, my mother is in the car. She
didn't think she could come in." The
mother was crying for joy as her
wheelchair was pushed up the ramp into
the mansion.

Thanks to the efforts of nearly 80 china painters from across the state, members of the Oklahoma World Organization of China Painters, the first lady received a special gift of 26 place settings of hand painted "Oklahoma Wildflower" china. The unique china depicted many of the wildflowers native or indigenous to Oklahoma's hills and roadsides. Here the china is shown with the state silver pattern, Windham, produced by the Tiffany Silver Company of New York City. The Nighs also added a set of gold electroplated dinnerware to supplement the silver pattern. Courtesy Oklahoma Publishing Company.

The weekly opening of the mansion was extremely popular. By 1982, 20,000 people visited the mansion annually.

At first Mrs. Nigh stayed at the mansion and visited with guests but people stopping to talk to her held up the line of visitors. After a few weeks, she ran errands away from the mansion during open houses.

The first lady was proud of the pieces of Oklahoma history she elegantly displayed in the various rooms of the mansion. Among the mementoes were items owned by each of the state's former governors, including Governor William J. Holloway's gavel, Robert S. Kerr's Bible, and David Boren's broom. In the official dining room was the silver punch bowl from the battleship USS *Oklahoma,* sunk during the attack on Pearl Harbor December 7, 1941. To encourage appreciation of Oklahoma artists, the Nighs displayed native art work throughout the mansion. The collection grew as the Nighs' scheduling secretaries encouraged civic clubs and organizations to which the governor or first lady addressed to break tradition. It was suggested that, rather than the presentation of a certificate or plaque, the Nighs be presented a piece of local art to display in the mansion. This plan furthered the Nighs' desire to promote Oklahoma artists.

The first lady believed her first obligation, after being a wife to her husband and a mother to her two children, was the full-time job as Oklahoma's first lady, overseeing the mansion and the three-member domestic staff. She said, "I must be the right kind of help to George." However, Mrs. Nigh wanted to have her own life also, to be casually independent, saying, "I don't want to depend on George for everything."

In the beginning, Mrs. Nigh, who had always cleaned her own house and cooked the family meals, thought taxpayers' money was being squandered by hiring cooks and cleaning staff at the mansion. It was not long until she changed her mind. She said, "Sometimes we have 20 for breakfast, 40 for lunch, and 80 for dinner. I felt like I was running a catering service. There is no way I could have done it by myself."

Doretha Hays, hired at the mansion during the Boren administration, became a valued friend and helper for Mrs. Nigh. Doretha, who served five governors, died in 1995. Doretha, who had three daughters herself, helped raise Georgeann. Doretha knew what to expect from visitors coming to the mansion. The first lady called her a "nurturing woman."

Mrs. Nigh's first luncheon as the new first lady was anything but peaceful. For some reason, fire alarms began blaring during the luncheon. No fire was found but huge, red fire trucks sat strategically placed around the mansion for the remainder of the afternoon.

Early in the new administration, the Nighs hosted a press luncheon at the mansion. The luncheon was scheduled to kick off the Wednesday open houses. After members of the press were seated, there was a late arrival, whom no one recognized. The man was not a member of the press, just a visitor who had arrived early for the open house scheduled for later in the day. Security guards thought he was a reporter and escorted him to the third floor luncheon. After the meal, the governor stood at the door of the state ballroom, shaking hands with reporters. Then the unknown guest whispered encouraging words to Nigh, "Thanks for the meal. I didn't know you were serving each week. You'll have a lot more people next week at open house, especially when I tell my friends."

Mrs. Nigh opened the governor's mansion to television viewers each December. The Oklahoma Educational Television Authority (OETA) broadcast a half-hour show entitled *From Our House to Your House*, with seasons greetings from the Nigh family.

Mrs. Nigh saw her role as first lady as an opportunity to further programs to serve Oklahoma's handicapped citizens. Years before, at the request of Governor Bartlett, during tours of state facilities, the Nighs visited the three state schools for the developmentally disabled. After seeing conditions at Pauls Valley, Enid, and Sand Springs, Mrs. Nigh resolved to dedicate her public work for these Oklahomans with special needs. From this humbling beginning, the first lady continued her efforts over the years, culminating in her appointment by President Bill Clinton in 1997 to the President's Committee on Mental Retardation.

Mrs. Nigh actively sought information about treatment and assessment of mentally retarded citizens. Ultimately, the first lady's lobbying of the Oklahoma legislature resulted in the creation of Donna Nigh Group Homes, a

A swimming pool in the shape of Oklahoma was added to the mansion grounds during the Nigh years. Loyd Benefield of Oklahoma City and Julian Rothbaum of Tulsa spearheaded a drive to raise $25,000 in contributions to finance the construction of the pool. Courtesy Oklahoma Publishing Company.

Above: First Lady Donna Nigh used leaded glass doors that previously covered bookshelves in the mansion library for folding screens on either side of the fireplace in the music room. Courtesy Jim Argo.

Below: One of the most treasured antiques in the mansion is Maximilian's bed, showcased in the second-floor guest bedroom. A popcorn-stitch crocheted coverlet came to Oklahoma in the Run of 1889. The roll top desk in the corner was a favorite of Governor Nigh. It was once owned by pioneer showman Pawnee Bill. Both the bed and desk were on loan from the Oklahoma Historical Society. Courtesy Oklahoma Publishing Company.

The formal library of the mansion, with its mix of Oriental and traditional decorating themes, was a popular place for entertaining. The setting overlooked the south and west lawns of the mansion and afforded a view of the State Capitol. Courtesy Oklahoma Publishing Company.

series of state-funded community alternatives to placing mentally retarded citizens in nursing homes. Mrs. Nigh's lobbying efforts were carried out while she helped prepare and serve breakfast to legislative leaders at the mansion on Tuesday mornings during the session.

In 1983 the Commission on Developmental Disabilities of the United States Department of Health chose Mrs. Nigh as Oklahoma's "Volunteer of the Year."

The following year many of Mrs. Nigh's friends established The Donna Nigh Foundation to provide funds to supplement the needs of Oklahoma's developmentally disabled.

A garage sale at the governor's mansion netted more than $20,000 for the foundation. Clowns, soft drinks, ice cream, beer, popcorn, peanuts, and cotton candy were included in the $25 gate admission. Once inside, buyers were faced with table after table of Nigh mementoes cleaned out of closets and drawers. Included were pieces of furniture and bud vases, t-shirts, and the keys to two Oklahoma towns, Broken Arrow and Woodward.

Other programs in which Mrs. Nigh was involved included preschool immunization campaigns and legislation to require approved car seats for children. Her pet project, however, was an annual Easter egg hunt for blind children. Held on the mansion grounds, Mrs. Nigh hosted students from the School for the Blind in Muskogee and other public and private schools and institutions serving blind children. Costumed characters such as Mr. and Mrs. Easter Bunny were on hand to assist the children. Huge baskets of candy, cookies, and toys were given to the children.

With the help of the Pioneers, a group of retired employees of Southwestern Bell Telephone Company, blind children hunted for plastic eggs that contained beepers, enabling them to locate the eggs. All the children, including those who had partial sight, were blindfolded to make the egg hunt fair. Sights such as the one of children scampering around the governor's mansion lawn looking for beeping eggs filled Mrs. Nigh's bright blue eyes with emotion and made a deep impact upon her life and her sense of doing something good for the people of Oklahoma.

Mrs. Nigh and her husband had to make time to be alone. They exercised regularly together, played tennis, and swam. Sundays were set aside as family and church day at Council Road Baptist Church.

None of Mrs. Nigh's jobs was more important than being a mother to Georgeann, who turned 14 just six days after her father was inaugurated as governor in January, 1979. The first lady laughingly predicted to reporters the difficulties Georgeann would encounter as a

One of the most interesting of the statewide Diamond Jubilee projects to celebrate Oklahoma's 75th birthday in 1982 was the making of a Diamond Jubilee quilt. First Lady Donna Nigh oversaw the completion of the quilt that contained a square from every county in the state. On May 12, 1981, women from around the state gathered at the governor's mansion to piece the squares together. It was exactly 50 years after the 1931 quilting bee hosted by First Lady Alice Murray. Courtesy Oklahoma Heritage Association.

teenager in the governor's mansion, "She's worried when she gets old enough to date, her dates will be afraid to come meet her daddy and the security guards, too." Mrs. Nigh said that her goal was to make Georgeann's life as near to normal as possible, although both she and Nigh recognized the near impossibility of achieving complete normalcy.

Georgeann was a sprightly blonde, an eighth grader at Western Oaks Junior High School near the Nigh's former home. She was a straight-A student who had proved her excellence in athletics since elementary school. She played guard on three basketball teams, was a top-notch softball player, played piano, and was a member of her school's pep club.

Even after moving into the governor's mansion, the Nighs made frequent trips to basketball gyms and softball fields to watch Georgeann play. A new addition to the governor's mansion grounds was a basketball goal.

Georgeann developed close friendships with security and household staff at the mansion. If her mother and father were away on official business, Georgeann often went to the guard shack and watched television with security officers on duty.

Being the daughter of the governor had its low moments. After an anonymous bomb threat during debate over Oklahoma's beer-drinking age in 1982, she had to stand outside the mansion in her bathing suit for hours while officers searched the executive residence. She had to change her private telephone number after reporters discovered the number and called her in the middle of the night asking for her father.

Mike Mashburn did not move to the mansion with his parents and Georgeann, having earlier left the nest after graduating from Putnam City West High School in 1970. He graduated from Oklahoma State University with a B.A. in marketing. He successfully entered the residential and commercial construction business.

The first family on inauguration day, 1979. Left to right, Mike Mashburn, Georgeann Nigh, Governor George Nigh, First Lady Donna Nigh. Courtesy Oklahoma Publishing Company.

In December, 1981, Mike married Mara Kerr, the granddaughter of the late United States Senator Robert S. Kerr, and daughter of Mr. and Mrs. William G. Kerr of Norman. Mike and Mara married in the Blue Room at the State Capitol, a marriage referred to by *The Daily Oklahoman* as "a Sooner version of a royal wedding." A reception at the governor's mansion followed.

After Mike and Mara were divorced, Mike moved into the garage apartment at the governor's mansion. The garage apartment was also home during the Nigh administration to former first lady Jeannette Edmondson. For a year, Mrs. Edmondson, who was Oklahoma's Secretary of State at the time, lived in the apartment while waiting to move into a new home.

Nigh served Oklahoma well during his eight-year stretch as governor from 1979 to 1987. As a former member of the Oklahoma House of Representatives and Lieutenant Governor, he worked closely with the legislature during the best and worst of economic times. In his first term, state revenues hit all time highs. But in his second term, falling oil and gas prices cut deeply into state government's income and resulted in budget cuts and large tax increases. Many believed Nigh's steady hand during the economic downturn prevented long range damage to the Oklahoma economy.

As governor, Nigh increased minority representation on state boards and commissions and in state agency management positions. He also appointed the first two women justices to the Oklahoma Supreme Court. He led unprecedented state efforts in highway construction and improving Oklahoma's penal system.

Nigh served as President of the University of Central Oklahoma, formerly Central State University, after his eight years as governor. Mrs. Nigh continued her work for Oklahoma's developmentally disabled population.

For more information on the George Nigh family, see:

Burke, Bob. *Good Guys Wear White Hats: The Life of George Nigh* (Oklahoma City: Oklahoma Heritage Association, 2000)

State carpenters used leftover shingles and lumber from other projects to build a house for the Nigh family dogs in 1985.

IN 1980, HENRY BELLMON VOLUNTARILY RETIRED FROM HIS SEAT IN THE UNITED STATES SENATE TO HIS FARM AT BILLINGS, OKLAHOMA. HOWEVER, BELLMON'S DESIRE FOR PUBLIC SERVICE RESULTED IN HIS ELECTION FOR A SECOND TIME AS GOVERNOR OF OKLAHOMA IN 1986. THE SECOND TERM AS GOVERNOR WOULD BE BELLMON'S FINAL TOUR OF ELECTED PUBLIC SERVICE DUTY AND IN BELLMON STYLE, IT WOULD NOT BE EASY OR QUIET.

THE BELLMONS A SECOND TIME

Henry Bellmon was elected governor of Oklahoma a second time in 1986 after serving as United States Senator from Oklahoma. He and First Lady Shirley Bellmon are the only first couple in state history to live in the governor's mansion at two different times. Courtesy Gail Bellmon Wynne.

IT WAS A FINAL LESSON in Bellmon leadership: determine where the public interests lie and lead in that direction, irrespective of temporary swings in public opinion. Major public school funding measures were passed during the second Bellmon term. Bellmon continued his efforts to make state government more efficient.

A new generation had been added to the Bellmon family in the 24 years since their first term began in 1963. Grandsons Brok, Ben, and Elliott led the Pledge of Allegiance at the inaugural ceremony. A combined choir from the Bellmons' home church, First Presbyterian Church of Perry, and daughter Gail's church, First Presbyterian of Enid, provided musical inspiration. Sunshine blessed the warm afternoon of Bellmon's second inauguration in January, 1987.

First Lady Shirley Bellmon chose for her second inaugural gown a dress of raspberry tissue lame' and antique taffeta with an empire waist and jewel neckline. Unlike his previous inaugural ball, Governor Bellmon sported a black tuxedo. Inaugural dinners were held at Oklahoma City's Whitehall and Petroleum clubs. A black-tie crowd of more than 1,500 attended the $125-a-plate dinners. Later in the evening, the Governor's Gala was held in the atrium at Leadership Square and the First Lady's Ball was in full swing at the Skirvin Hotel Grand Ballroom. Dance floors were crowded to capacity at both locations.

Not long after the Bellmons moved into the governor's mansion a second time, the first lady was working in her second floor office dressed in pajamas and a robe when a group of visiting women decided to depart from the regular tour. When Mrs. Bellmon heard a few of the more curious women in the room next to the office, the first lady ducked into a closet. The women looked at her office and commented on the confused state of her desk, not knowing Mrs. Bellmon was hiding in the closet.

Mrs. Bellmon asked Sally Ferrell, the wife of Chandler newspaper publisher, Don Ferrell, to develop a new kind of public tour of the governor's mansion. The kitchen was added to the tour. Members of county and city historical

Below: Governor Henry Bellmon and First Lady Shirley Bellmon welcome Edward L. Gaylord, right, and Mr. and Mrs. Henry Cannon, left. Mrs. Cannon was better known as Minnie Pearl. Courtesy Oklahoma Publishing Company.

Left: The three grandsons of Henry and Shirley Bellmon led the Pledge of Allegiance at the 1987 inauguration of their grandfather. Left to right, Ben Cooper McFerron, Brok Adam McFerron, and Elliott Bellmon Wynne. Courtesy Gail Bellmon Wynne.

Facing page: An early winter snowstorm
dropped seven inches of snow on the mansion
in December, 1987, creating a beautiful setting.
Courtesy Fred Marvel.

Left: The hall mirror was part of the original
furnishings of the governor's mansion in 1928.
Courtesy Jim Argo.

Below: The Bellmons chose a blue leather couch
for the mansion library. Courtesy Jim Argo.

societies served as tour guides from 1:00 P.M to 3:00 P.M. each Wednesday. Dr. Bob Blackburn of the Oklahoma Historical Society prepared fact sheets about the mansion for distribution to tour guides.

Mrs. Bellmon complimented the excellent condition of the mansion after the Nigh family had lived there for eight years. However, some changes were in store. The first project was to take up the carpet in the grand foyer, exposing the hardwood floor. Later all the floors in the downstairs of the mansion were refinished and the kitchen was remodeled. The leaded-glass doors were reinstalled on the library shelves. The first lady took a special class in working with leaded glass to recreate the missing doors on shelves over the entrance to the dining room.

For her renovation efforts, the first lady was selected by the Oklahoma Historical Society for its George Shirk Award, given for outstanding historic preservation.

The Bellmon daughters and their husbands surprised the governor and first lady with a 40th wedding anniversary party in January, 1987. In typical Bellmon fashion it was a small dinner party of long time friends held in the first floor foyer of the mansion. An orchestra played while dinner was being served.

Pictures of former first families were displayed on both sides of the walls in the north entry of the mansion. The project was commissioned by First Lady Shirley Bellmon and paid for by the Oklahoma Historical Society. At right is Henry S. Johnston's hall tree and the state seal etched in the glass door. Courtesy Oklahoma Historical Society.

In August, 1990, the Bellmons hosted a First Families Reunion for descendants of Oklahoma's governors. More than 40 members of first families attended the event at the mansion. The Oklahoma Historical Society assisted the first lady in locating relatives of Oklahoma chief executives. Children of different administrations exchanged stories in rooms that were once their own. Gail Bellmon Wynne remembered, "Dinner was served outside under a tent where favorite memories of the house were shared. Pictures were snapped and new memories were made for new generations."

While much of Mrs. Bellmon's time during her first stay in the governor's mansion had been devoted to her children, in the second term she was free to involve herself in diverse activities. Her interest in stained glass and other crafts resulted in an annual bazaar appropriately dubbed the "First Lady's Bazaar" that drew up to 100 exhibitors and thousands of visitors to the Harn Museum grounds in Oklahoma City.

Mrs. Bellmon's work on the annual bazaar convinced her that many women were interested in home-based businesses to supplement family income. She worked with Oklahoma State University to develop home business conferences in all sections of the state. During a national education conference, First Lady Barbara Bush invited Mrs. Bellmon and home extension leaders from OSU to the White House to discuss home-based businesses with reporters. The meeting resulted in a number of news stories about Mrs. Bellmon's efforts.

The first lady developed a line of dolls called the "First Lady's Collection," first shown at the Dallas, Texas gift market in the summer of 1990, where orders for 3,000 were taken. She developed the "Shir-Lee" line of dresses, a shirt waist dress made of pure silk, appliquéd with state symbols.

The first lady assisted the "Don't Lay that Trash on Oklahoma" anti-litter campaign and promoted the planting of wildflowers along Oklahoma's highways. Wildflower seeds were grown and harvested by prison inmates. Mrs. Bellmon and other state officials appeared in print and television advertisements to promote the anti-litter campaign.

Another program benefited from Mrs. Bellmon's dedication. The Oklahoma Alliance Against Drug Abuse was formed to battle drug use within the state.

But life at the mansion was not all work. Family and friends continued to play an important part in the life of Henry and Shirley Bellmon. Grandsons Brok, Ben, and Elliott were soon joined by the arrival of the fourth grandson Will. Summers brought daughter Ann and her boys, Brok and Ben, for extended vacations from their home in Maryland. The mansion invasion would be complete when Elliott and Gail arrived from Enid and Will and Pat from Billings. The boys loved visiting the guard shack and hanging out with the guards. One guard even confessed to making his rounds on Elliott's skateboard.

The west entryway to the central hall gave a good view of the original chandeliers that once hung in the formal dining room. Courtesy Jim Argo.

Right: The living room was decorated for Christmas by First Lady Shirley Bellmon. Courtesy Jim Argo.

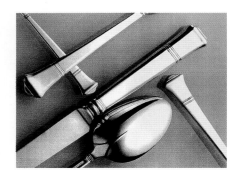

Above: Tiffany silver has been used in the mansion dining room since the years of First Lady Ethel Johnston. This is the Windham pattern first shown by Tiffany & Co. in New York City in 1923. Courtesy Tiffany & Co.

Right: The china on the mansion dining room table by Lenox features a gold band and state seal on a cream-colored background. The china was used with gold-plated flatware purchased during the Nigh administration. The crystal coordinates with a simple gold band. Courtesy Jim Argo.

Paneling was removed from the former family dining room and former guardroom to reveal a mural hung during the Edmondson years. Courtesy Oklahoma Historical Society.

After his second term as governor, Bellmon and his first lady retired again to their Billings farm. Mrs. Bellmon operated her doll-making business from a former hardware store in Billings and helped recreate dresses for a collection of dresses and gowns of Oklahoma's First Ladies.

In his autobiography, Governor Bellmon described the first lady, "She is a woman of focus—She helped raise three daughters who are members of the generation of women whose choices are unlimited, while her generation was caught in the transition between traditional roles and nontraditional ones. It wasn't always easy, but Shirley has made the transition. She raised a family and was a political wife in a time when it was still important to be a traditional political wife. Then, she became one of those in her generation to break out of those roles. I have always been proud of her, but never more than I am today."

Mrs. Bellmon died of a heart attack July 24, 2000, while on a family vacation in Cape Cod, Massachusetts. First Lady Cathy Keating said, "If there is an enduring model of what a first lady should be, it is the example set by Shirley Bellmon."

For more information on the Henry Bellmon family, see:

Bellmon, Henry with Pat Bellmon. *The Life and Times of Henry Bellmon* (Tulsa: Council Oak Books, 1992)

Below: First Lady Rhonda Walters, in her blue inaugural dress, and Governor David Walters. Courtesy David and Rhonda Walters.

Facing page: The governor and first lady pose with children, left to right, Kristen, Shaun, Elizabeth, and Tanna, for a family photograph during early December, 1991. Courtesy David and Rhonda Walters.

Special note: The authors express their appreciation to David and Rhonda Walters for writing this chapter.

OKLAHOMA DEMOCRATS REGAINED CONTROL OF THE GOVERNOR'S MANSION IN 1990 WITH THE ELECTION OF DAVID LEE WALTERS, WHO CARRIED 75 OF THE STATE'S 77 COUNTIES IN THE GENERAL ELECTION WITH A 35-YEAR RECORD FOR MARGIN OF VICTORY.

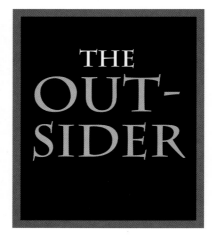

THE OUT-SIDER

WALTERS was born November 20, 1951, near Canute, Oklahoma, raised on a small cotton and wheat farm, and graduated as valedictorian of Canute High School in 1969. He earned an industrial engineering degree from the University of Oklahoma and his Master of Business Administration from Harvard University.

The election of Walters signaled a desire of the public to elect a real out-sider. Since the election of Robert S. Kerr nearly a half century before, no other governor had been elected who had not previously held elective public office. Walters began his professional career as an administrator at the University of Oklahoma and then entered private business as head of two real estate companies. Governor Nigh asked him to co-chair the 100-member Commission on Government Reform in 1984 and later appointed him to serve on the Oklahoma Human Services Commission.

Walters failed in his first bid for the governor's office in 1986, losing to Republican Henry Bellmon after winning the Democratic nomination. In 1990, Walters campaigned on a platform of no new taxes without public approval, his promise to run state government like a business, his support for term limits, and his support for education reforms.

Major capital improvements were made on Oklahoma's higher education campuses during the Walters administration. Walters launched major initiatives in children's, rural development, and welfare reform programs. His "Quality Jobs" program was called the most aggressive job incentive package in the nation by *U.S. News and World Report*. He successfully sponsored significant workers' compensation reform. A leading technology magazine recognized Walters as the nation's leading governor in the introduction of technology to government applications.

Right: Governor David Walters embraces son, Shaun, on his 20th birthday, December 8, 1991. Watching gleefully are sisters Kristen, left, and Elizabeth. Courtesy David and Rhonda Walters.

Below: First Lady Rhonda Walters. Courtesy Stuart Ostler.

David met Rhonda Smith of Elk City the summer after they both graduated from high school in 1969. During high school they lived only seven miles from each other but had never met. One summer evening in 1969, David dropped his parents off to visit relatives in Elk City. Cruising Main Street, from the Sonic Drive-In to the Safeway parking lot, David met Rhonda and was smitten enough to forget that he was supposed to pick up his parents two hours earlier.

David and Rhonda enrolled at the University of Oklahoma. They dated two years before marrying in 1971. Rhonda left college to work for the City of Norman to help David complete his engineering degree. She later obtained a real estate broker's license and established a successful real estate career.

The future first lady loved children, served briefly as a substitute elementary teacher, and was the doting new mom for Shaun, followed by Tanna, Kristen, and Elizabeth.

The Walters held ten special events to mark their inauguration on January 14, 1991. They included four inaugural preludes in different areas of the state: Enid, Lawton, McAlester, and Canute. On Saturday before the Monday inauguration, the first lady's Inaugural Dinner and Ball was held at the Doubletree Hotel in Tulsa.

A Children's Inaugural was the highlight of activities at the Capitol the day before the inauguration, an attempt to emphasize Mrs. Walters' wish that children's issues be a priority in the Walters administration. Dancers, clowns, mimes, storytellers, and a play, *The Three Billy Goats Gruff*, brought over 5,000 children to the Capitol. The Oklahoma Institute for Child Advocacy and the Inaugural Committee sponsored the event.

Right: By opening up previously closed windows and introducing brick floors, wood inset ceilings, Oklahoma granite counter tops, and all new appliances, the kitchen was returned to its original form and was made very functional. Interior designer Rand Elliott of Oklahoma City oversaw the installation of elegant glass cabinets that made the kitchen a showplace. Courtesy Jim Argo.

Above left: First Lady Rhonda Walters removed a wall and combined two rooms to make a larger upstairs family room. This photograph shows the work area where Mrs. Walters could attend to her official duties and be with her children at the same time.

Left: At the opposite end of the room a door opened to an outside deck. Courtesy Jim Argo.

Top: A sewing and breakfast room was converted into a study for the governor on the first floor of the mansion. The rich mahogany paneling added during First Lady Rhonda Walters' renovation provided Governor Walters a comfortable place for small meetings. Courtesy Jim Argo.

Bottom: To add more privacy to the family quarters, First Lady Rhonda Walters had a door closed off on the second floor foyer creating this beautiful setting at the second floor landing. Courtesy Jim Argo.

Five thousand guests joined the new governor and first lady at an inaugural ball at Oklahoma City's Kirkpatrick Center. Former Governor George Nigh was the master of ceremonies and introduced the first couple who danced solo to their requested song, *Wind Beneath My Wings*, played by the Al Good Orchestra. Then state and campaign officials took to the dance floor in their tuxedos and evening gowns.

During the first week in the governor's mansion, the Walters hosted 13 events for more than 1,000 guests. The mansion staff politely suggested that perhaps they should slow the pace down.

First Lady Rhonda Walters began an aggressive campaign to renovate the mansion in early 1991. Interior designers and architects worked out plans to remodel and expand an outdated kitchen, prepare a study on the first floor of the mansion for the governor, and freshen up the downstairs. Private donors to the Walters Inaugural Fund agreed to the use of surplus funds to help finance the renovation.

The mansion library was warm and inviting to visitors. First Lady Rhonda Walters wanted the mansion to be a comfortable home for both the first family and the thousands of official visitors who trekked to the executive residence each year. Courtesy Jim Argo.

For the four Walters children came an update of their bedrooms. The first couple's master bedroom closets were expanded and the master bathroom was updated with a whirlpool tub, a new all-glass shower, and a new Oklahoma granite vanity.

Two rooms were combined to make the family room larger. The first lady wanted to be closer to her children so she placed her office at one end of the enlarged family room. By closing a door on the second floor, an intimate second-floor landing was created.

First Lady Shirley Bellmon had begun to remove carpet to expose the handsome wood floors, and the Walters completed the project by sanding and refinishing the remaining wood floors. The Walters moved newly purchased furniture into the mansion to supplement the existing furnishings.

The former music room served as a formal living room where Governor Walters conducted meetings. Courtesy Jim Argo.

Elizabeth Walters' bedroom in the mansion was a typical four-year-old's bedroom, complete with stuffed animals and a doll carriage. Courtesy Jim Argo.

To obtain additional funding to operate and maintain the mansion, First Lady Rhonda Walters seized an opportunity one evening at the mansion to lobby State Senator Stratton Taylor of Claremore. While listening to the first lady's presentation, Taylor leaned back in one of the aging chairs in the mansion dining room. The chair gave way and Taylor lay on the floor in a pile of wood that formerly was his chair. Taylor quickly conceded the need for a budget increase for the mansion although he kiddingly suggested the chair had been "doctored."

An exit onto an upstairs deck or sun porch was improved and the deck repaired during Rhonda Walters' renovation. This lovely spot was a frequent stop for a light lunch during a busy day. Courtesy Jim Argo.

The renovation of the kitchen, master bed and bath, garage apartment, the creation of a new family room and downstairs study, and a general cosmetic update of other areas provided the first family a lovely and comfortable official residence.

Mrs. Walters had a seven-foot grand piano on loan from the Oklahoma Historical Society refinished for the music room. The three oldest Walters children played the piano.

When the Walters family moved into the mansion their oldest child, Shaun, was attending the University of Oklahoma and lived on campus. However, when he came home on weekends to the mansion, his two youngest sisters doubled up to provide him a bedroom.

Kristen was ten and attended John Carroll School. Elizabeth, age four, occupied a bedroom filled with a menagerie of stuffed animals and dolls. Oldest daughter, Tanna, attended McGuiness High School and slept in an oversized Victorian bed that reportedly belonged to Empress Carlotta of Mexico, the wife of the Emperor Maximillian. The bed was on loan from the Oklahoma Historical Society.

The first lady was very active in children's advocacy projects. She appeared in radio and television public service announcements in a Due by Two program that provided free immunization shots to children less than two years of age. Her efforts contributed to a stunning increase in the number of immunizations for children in Oklahoma that previously had one of the worst records for early childhood immunizations in the country.

Children were to have been the focus of the Walters' first Christmas in the mansion. More than 100 dolls, donated by Attic Babies, decorated five Christmas trees in the mansion and recently renovated garage quarters. Each of the cuddly characters was for sale with the proceeds donated to the Children's Convalescent Center in Bethany and Children's Medical Research. Students from Oklahoma State University-Oklahoma City decorated the living room and the master bedroom with white and pastel-colored poinsettias donated from the college's greenhouse.

Tragedy struck the Walters family however during the holiday season. In the middle of press attacks and controversy surrounding his father, Shaun Walters' apartment in Norman was the subject of a search by police who found a single seed in a closet and a water pipe stored for a friend. Prosecutors, under great pressure not to show favoritism to the governor's son, attempted to get a possession of drug paraphernalia charge filed. Shaun voluntarily took drug tests that showed no evidence of drug usage.

Heavy press coverage followed the sprouting of the seed which turned out not to be marijuana. However, family members and friends believed psychological damage was done. Governor Walters later recalled, "Press coverage was so intense that Shaun had to crawl

Above: First Lady Rhonda Walters authored a cookbook while she lived in the mansion. A portion of the proceeds of the sale of the cookbook went to children's medical research. The photograph for the book's cover was taken by Jim Argo. Courtesy Jim Argo.

through a back window of his apartment to avoid a television stake out." The pressure was too much for the 20-year-old who took an overdose of medication he had been prescribed for a reflux condition. He died 11 days later on December 26, 1991.

Understandably, the Walters family was devastated and all Oklahomans mourned the loss. Shaun's death changed Governor Walters' outlook on political life. Asked if he would run for governor if he had it to do all over again, Walters replied, "No, I would not. I lost my son because I ran for public office."

After a long absence from the public eye, Mrs. Walters invited 200 schoolchildren to the Capitol in March, 1993, to publicize 13 initiatives for Oklahoma children. The proposals ranged from comprehensive health education to childhood poverty. Over 75 percent of these action items were accomplished through legislative or executive action.

The first lady was the spokesperson for the "Healthy Futures" campaign, a public education and awareness initiative to place the issues of child abuse, prenatal and child health, and child care development before Oklahoma citizens.

For her work on children's issues, First Lady Rhonda Walters was honored by many groups, including the University of Oklahoma College of Public Health Alumni Association and the Oklahoma Association of Children Under Six. She also was presented the first annual Betty Blake Rogers Award by the Oklahoma Kids organization for exemplifying the spirit of the wife of Oklahoma humorist Will Rogers.

In order to honor the memory of their late son and children of all Oklahoma governors, the Walters commissioned in 1994 a bronze sculpture to be placed on the mansion grounds to honor children of past, present, and future Oklahoma governors. The red granite base of the sculpture includes the names of all the children of Oklahoma chief executives. The youngest Walters daughter, Elizabeth, was a model for the girl and the boy in the sculpture was modeled after Shaun. Private donations, assisted by former governors Boren and Nigh, funded the $50,000 sculpture by Lena Beth Frazier of Norman.

After three years of investigation of alleged campaign contribution irregularities and "fearing that the continued negative attacks could further damage his family," lawyers for Governor Walters negotiated with prosecutors to end the process. An agreement was reached that the governor would plead guilty to a misdemeanor offense and pay a fine and the record would be expunged in 12 months. Walters claimed his innocence but said it was in the best interest of the state and his family to accept the plea agreement.

Walters entered the international independent power business after his term as governor. He served on the executive committee of the Oklahoma Academy and was active in a variety of charitable fundraising efforts.

After leaving the mansion, Mrs. Walters continued her career in real estate and volunteer work for Oklahoma education and children's advocacy. She raised money in her son's name for both her church, Our Lady's Cathedral Parish, and for the Department of Pediatrics at the University of Oklahoma Health Sciences Center. In 1999, she was appointed by President Bill Clinton to the Commission on Presidential Scholars, a national program that annually recognizes outstanding graduating seniors.

A week before Frank Keating was sworn in as governor, two first families gathered around the mansion sculpture honoring past and present children of Oklahoma governors. Left to right, governor-elect Frank Keating, Carrie Keating, Kelly Keating, Chip Keating, Kristen Walters, Cathy Keating, Tanna Walters, First Lady Rhonda Walters, Governor David Walters, and Elizabeth Walters, front row. The sculpture was a gift of the Walters family. Courtesy Oklahoma Publishing Company.

Frank and Cathy Keating prepare to welcome guests to the housewarming for the governor's mansion in March, 1995. Courtesy Michael Ives and Ackerman McQueen.

acing page: The first family, 1998. Left to right, Chip Keating, Carrie Keating, First Lady Cathy Keating, Governor Frank Keating, and Kelly Keating. Courtesy Frank and Cathy Keating.

A HOUSE WORTH SAVING

THE AGING EXECUTIVE RESIDENCE had seen good times and bad. As First Lady Cathy Keating prepared to move her family into the mansion in January, 1995, Mrs. Keating described the mansion as a baton in a relay race, handed off from first family to first family. It was time for a major facelift for Oklahoma's governor's mansion.

Governor Keating was born February 2, 1944, in St. Louis, Missouri. His father was an oil field roughneck who moved to Tulsa to form his own oil company. Young Keating was a student leader throughout high school at Tulsa Cascia Hall, at Georgetown University, where he majored in English, history, and economics, and the University of Oklahoma School of Law.

After graduation from law school, Keating became an FBI agent. Two years later he was named Assistant District Attorney for Tulsa County. In 1972 Keating jumped into politics and was elected to the Oklahoma House of Representatives from Tulsa. Four days after he was sworn in, he married pretty Catherine Dunn Heller, born in Tulsa on September 18, 1950. They had met just seven months before on a blind date set up by Cathy's former college roommate. When Cathy discovered the future governor was 28 years old, she remarked, "I'll have to ask my mother. I am not sure she will let me go out with you. I'm only 21."

The future first lady had strong Oklahoma roots. Her great-grandparents came to the state in the land run of 1893. One grandfather was an oil wildcatter. Another co-founded Skelly Oil Company. A great-uncle, Jesse Dunn, was the first chief justice of the Oklahoma Supreme Court. Cathy graduated from the University of Oklahoma with a degree in elementary education.

Cathy was six years younger than Frank but discovered that this "man of the world" had grown up two blocks from her. By their third date, Cathy and Frank were talking of marriage. Cathy, an Episcopalian, converted to Catholicism to join her husband in raising a future family in that faith.

The Keatings' first child, Carrie, arrived less than a year later. Two years later, Kelly was born. And four years after that, fifth-generation Francis Anthony Keating, III, nicknamed "Chip," arrived.

Keating served in the Oklahoma legislature from 1972 to 1981. He was appointed United States Attorney for the Northern District of Oklahoma in 1981. He practiced law in Tulsa from 1983 until he joined the Reagan administration in 1985 as Assistant Secretary of the Treasury, supervising the Customs Service; Secret Service; and the Bureau of Alcohol, Tobacco, and Firearms. He also served as Associate Attorney General under President Ronald Reagan and Acting Deputy Secretary and General Counsel of the United States Department of Housing and Urban Development in the administration of President George Bush.

In 1993 Keating returned to Oklahoma and was elected governor the following year. His campaign was based on calls for tax cuts, a right to work law, and reform of the state's workers' compensation system. The Keating campaign theme was "Oklahoma ONE: opportunity, neighborhood, education." Keating pledged to push Oklahoma to catch up with the economies of other states.

Above: The governor and First Lady examine china given by donors in 1995 to permanently furnish the mansion. Courtesy Oklahoma Publishing Company.

Right: First Lady Cathy Keating holds a Rosenthal pattern teacup and plate, part of a set of china at the governor's mansion. Each piece was painted by Oklahoma artists and displays Oklahoma wildflowers. The set was commissioned during the Nigh administration and fired under the direction of an Oklahoma china painters group. Courtesy Oklahoma Publishing Company.

A replica of the sterling silver punch bowl originally commissioned for use on the battleship USS *Oklahoma* was unveiled in December, 1996. Left to right, First Lady Cathy Keating, Governor Frank Keating, Oklahoma Historical Society President Dr. Marvin Kroeker, and Dr. Michael Izrael, the New York City silversmith who created the replica.

The original service, designed by Walter Dean of Oklahoma City was one of a kind and valued at over $600,000. It was two feet long and over 18 inches tall, with an eight-gallon capacity. It weighed 67 pounds. The state seal of Oklahoma is cast in relief on one side; the other is an engraving of the 1889 land run. On one end is a bust of Sequoyah and, on the opposite end, is Captain David Payne, leader of the Boomers, who agitated for the opening of the Unassigned Lands to white settlement. The silver service was saved only because it had been removed for repairs when the battleship was sunk during the December 6, 1941 attack on Pearl Harbor.

Damage caused by heavy usage of the original punch bowl caused historical preservationists to call for the creation of a replica. The reproduction is now loaned on an annual basis to the governor's mansion by the Oklahoma Historical Society. The replica was paid for by private donations from Edna Hoffman Bowman of Kingfisher, the Robert S. and Grayce B. Kerr Foundation, the Oklahoma City Chapter of the Navy League of the United States, and the Oklahoma Veterans Council. The original punch bowl is on display at the Oklahoma Historical Society. Courtesy Fred Marvel.

Before Keating's inauguration, Mrs. Keating scheduled lunches with several former First Ladies, seeking their knowledge on how first families could survive their time in the mansion. Toward the end of a lunch with Ann Bartlett, the former first lady reached into her purse and handed Mrs. Keating a tissue containing a gold charm with the likeness of St. Francis of Assissi. Governor Bartlett had given the charm to his wife on the morning of his inauguration to wear on her charm bracelet. It came with his wishes that the prayer of St. Francis be with her always as she traveled the state. Mrs. Bartlett was sending those same wishes to Mrs. Keating.

Facing page: Thousands of twinkling lights illuminate the governor's mansion at night, Christmas, 1998. Courtesy Stuart Ostler.

Left: The Oklahoma governor's mansion: Christmas 1995, by Oklahoma artist Nick Berry. The painting was used for the Keating's 1995 Christmas card. Courtesy Nick Berry.

Below: In 1997, Margaret Bruza designed a Christmas ornament depicting the mansion on its 70th anniversary. The ornament was the first of a series of collectibles. Sales benefit the Friends of the Mansion, Inc. Others were of the Phillips Pavillion and the Oklahoma State Flag, signifying the Sooner State's admission to the Union in 1907 as America's 46th state. Courtesy Margaret Bruza.

The Oklahoma Governor's Mansion

Little did Mrs. Bartlett know that Mrs. Keating had recited the prayer of St. Francis of Assissi nightly since childhood, and it was a guiding force in her life. The new first lady graciously accepted the gift and wore the charm as a necklace, beginning the morning of her husband's inauguration. Since that time, Mrs. Keating has seldom been seen without the charm. The first lady said, "There is a very special bond which is felt between First Ladies regardless of political party. This gift truly epitomizes the significance of that bond."

Mrs. Bartlett's children learned of the special gift when a reporter told the story as a special feature. Later, Joanie Bartlett Atkinson purchased a similar charm in Italy and gave it to her mother to replace the original given by her father.

Sold-out pre-inaugural balls in Ponca City, Lawton, and Tulsa preceded Keating's inauguration as the state's 25th governor on January 9, 1995. After the inauguration on the south steps of the State Capitol, the governor and first lady led the first dance at the inaugural ball that was held at the National Cowboy Hall of Fame in Oklahoma City. An

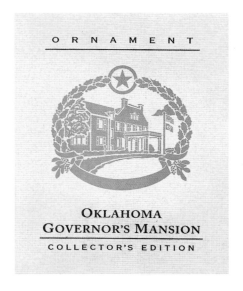

ORNAMENT

OKLAHOMA
GOVERNOR'S MANSION
COLLECTOR'S EDITION

estimated 10,000 persons attended the four inaugural ball events. Mrs. Keating's gown was an electric blue long dress embellished with a hand-embroidered state seal at the midriff. The full skirted dress was designed by Sherri Hill of Norman.

Chip Keating, 15, was the only child of the new first family to move into the mansion. Chip enrolled at Bishop McGuinness High School in Oklahoma City. Carrie, 21, was a junior foreign affairs and Spanish major at the University of Virginia and Kelly, 19, was a freshman at Southern Methodist University. In 2000, Carrie was a law student at the University of Oklahoma and married fellow student Ryan Leonard, the son of United States District Judge and Mrs. Tim Leonard. Carrie and Ryan held the wedding reception in the mansion gardens.

As with past first families moving into the mansion, the Keatings found very few permanent furnishings. After the Walters moved their personal furniture from the mansion, the executive residence was basically empty.

The new first lady scheduled an open house for the mansion for March 5, 1995, inviting Oklahomans to bring housewarming gifts to the mansion. Mrs. Keating's goal was to obtain furnishings that would remain permanently with the mansion, regardless of who was governor.

The first lady registered the mansion with leading furniture and department stores, making a detailed list of items needed to make the executive residence a suitable place to conduct the affairs of state. She wanted all Oklahomans, at every income level, to be able to give to the mansion project. Gifts ranged from $2.50 napkins to area rugs for the dining room and family room.

More than 2,500 people attended the housewarming. Visitors, often lined up 50 deep during the day, brought gifts including artwork, silver, china, a statute of a rooster, linens monogrammed with the state seal, quilts, cookbooks, a hand-carved eagle, antique silver and serving trays, a handcrafted clock, an old microscope, and a Native American doll.

Citizens of Chickasha brought a sparkling Montgolfier crystal chandelier. Earlier, 12-year-old Joe Max Freeman of Hobart gave first son Chip a champion-bloodline Labrador Retriever puppy for the mansion.

Doretha, the longtime housekeeper, mentioned to the first lady that hundreds of people had tripped over a certain step on the mansion stairs through the years, just after Mrs. Keating had tripped on that stair. Later during the renovation of the mansion, work crews could find nothing wrong with the step, leaving Mrs. Keating to wonder if the rumors that "Alfalfa Bill" Murray's ghost still lived in the mansion were true. Surely, the first lady mused, "Alfalfa Bill" must sit at the bottom of the stairs and trip people on purpose.

Oklahoma's worst nightmare occurred just 100 days into the Keating administration. On April 19, 1995, a bomb destroyed the Alfred P. Murrah Federal Office Building in downtown Oklahoma City. Suddenly, the new governor and first lady were thrust into the national and

Facing page: The mansion dining room table is filled to capacity for a Christmas buffet, 1998. Courtesy Stuart Ostler.

international spotlight. As a team they became spokespersons for the very soul of Oklahoma. Together they led drives to raise money to help the injured and to educate the orphans left behind by the tragedy. They translated Oklahoma's pain, grief, and compassion to the entire world. The first lady spearheaded the publication of *In Their Name*, a Random House book memorializing the stories of rescue workers, survivors, and families of victims of the Oklahoma City bombing. The book made the national best-seller list and raised more than $1 million for Project Recovery Inc., a non-profit group created to assist bombing victims and their families.

For their humanitarian efforts in the days and months following the Murrah Building bombing, the governor and first lady were presented the Salvation Army's most prestigious award, the William Booth Award.

During Keating's first term as governor, he orchestrated the largest tax cut in history, successfully recruited new business to Oklahoma, put together a $3 billion-five-year road building program, and brought about sweeping reform of the workers' compensation system.

In her first few months in the mansion, Mrs. Keating began to explore what other states had done with aging executive residences. She founded Friends of the Mansion, Inc., a private non-profit corporation that was committed to the preservation of the mansion and thus provide substantial private funding for its cosmetic upkeep and a mechanism for long-term inventory.

The historic Buttram estate, a 30-room palatial home in Nichols Hills, an exclusive suburb of Oklahoma City, was put up for sale in 1995. Members of the Buttram family suggested the state should buy the mansion for use as a governor's official residence. However, the Keatings never considered moving.

It was clear to the first lady that the mansion needed extensive renovation. The low-hanging ceiling at the top of the stairs caused many visitors to bang their heads. The roof leaked. The downstairs paneling needed to be restored to its original deep color and richness.

Decorators, after extensive historical research and review of hundreds of old photographs, searched for a central theme for the mansion. Decorators who assisted the project were Fanny Bolen, Stephen Edwards, Ann Henry, Vicki Hicks, Charles Faudree, Kay Duffy, John Fluitt, and Brenda Philips. The effort was chaired by Deby Snodgrass. The Oklahoma Historical Society was a consultant for the project, as was the Capitol Preservation Commission. The first lady, an advocate of historic preservation, emphasized painstaking restoration rather than wholesale renovation.

The Keatings wanted to put a sense of history back into the mansion. Thus, in the Oklahoma Room, a specially commissioned rug bore the state seal. A staircase runner listed every governor since statehood. Period photos, depicting past first families, decorated the walls of the third floor ballroom.

The mansion kitchen was gutted. New commercial appliances were installed to handle large receptions and dinner parties. A new cooling and heating system was added to the second and third floors. Ceilings were raised and roof and structural defects were repaired. The first family lived in the apartment over the mansion garage while major structural repairs were made to the mansion.

The $1 million mansion renovation, paid for with private donations, emphasized elegance and was completed in 1996. Taxpayer dollars were used for a few structural repairs. The original maple flooring of the upstairs ballroom was restored. A replica of the silver punch bowl of the USS *Oklahoma* sat on a table in the entry hall. Every room became a treasure chest. Mrs. Keating wrote, "The result is traditional elegance with something of the flavor of an English drawing room, splashed with Oklahoma themes and colors and dotted throughout with gifts donated by Oklahomans." The National Cowboy Hall of Fame and Western Heritage Center in Oklahoma City and the Gilcrease Museum in Tulsa loaned major works of art to adorn the mansion walls.

Aluminum windows were replaced with wooden windows. The red tile roof was repaired, the limestone exterior was renewed, and a dormer on the east side of the mansion was rebuilt. Plastic shutters were replaced and unsafe fireplaces were repaired. Original wood molding was gently restored to either its original rich walnut finish or a perfect state to be repainted. Plaster ceilings were covered with gypsum wallboard. The walnut paneling in the library and dining room was re-stained.

A sculpture of native son Will Rogers was placed on the library mantle. The master and guest bedrooms echoed soft, floral themes with a touch of lace. First son Chip's room told of his love for bird hunting.

Mrs. Keating's goal in furnishing the mansion was not to buy all new items. She searched the state for antiques, saying, "We don't want it to look like we went to a showroom. We want it to look like there's a sense of history here."

Several thousand people braved bone-chilling winds in early December, 1995, to get a look at the refurbished mansion. In 1996 regular weekly tours of the governor's mansion resumed. Oklahomans were breathless when they saw the incredible transformation of the executive residence.

Architectural Digest featured the mansion's renovation in its April, 1997 issue. The magazine called the mansion "one of Oklahoma's top tourist sites," noting that 50,000 people had visited within the first year of weekly tours. The *Architectural Digest* article said, "The finished work is remarkably true to its 1920 roots while also evoking a broader sweep of Oklahoma history; one particularly affecting detail is the half-dozen teddy bears scattered around the house, symbols of the millions donated to the youngest victims of the Oklahoma City bombing. Stately but welcoming, elegant but robust and quirky as the state's boom-and-bust history, the mansion has been transformed from generic blandness into an Oklahoma icon."

Left: The Mansion Foyer: Christmas 1996, by native Oklahoman James Steinmeyer. The Keatings used the painting for their 1996 Christmas card. Courtesy James Steinmeyer.

Below: The entrance to the First Ladies Rose Garden, 1998. Many of Oklahoma's First Ladies have cultivated roses on the grounds of the mansion. Courtesy Betty Crow.

Below: In 1998, the Phillips Pavilion, a spacious covered facility, was built east of the mansion with private donations. It contains twin fireplaces and a commercial kitchen to serve up to 225 guests for a sit-down dinner and 500 people for a reception. The construction of the Phillips Pavilion reduced the amount of taxpayer expense for rental of everything from chairs to flatware for large functions at the mansion. The Pavilion is also home to a gift shop, with all proceeds going to the Friends of the Mansion revolving fund for the preservation of the mansion and grounds. One of the first events hosted at the Phillips Pavilion was a statewide Mother's Day Tea. Courtesy Stuart Ostler.

First Lady Cathy Keating did far more for Oklahoma than just renovate the official executive residence. She and her husband actively supported programs to cut Oklahoma's high divorce rate. Mrs. Keating promoted awareness of women's health issues by hosting a 1997 conference at the mansion attended by women from 43 of Oklahoma's 77 counties. The goal of the Oklahoma Women's Health Network is to educate the public about symptoms and prevention in breast and cervical cancer, cardiovascular disease, menopause, mental health, and osteoporosis.

Mrs. Keating served on the board of the Children's Museum and Children's Medical Research Foundation, as an advisor to the National Trust for Historic Preservation, and was Honorary State Chair for the American Cancer Society's Project Woman. She was Honorary Chair of the Habitat for Humanity first-ever All Woman's Blitz Build in Oklahoma and serves on the Habitat for Humanity International Women's Advisory Board.

The first lady underwent three surgeries in six weeks in early 1997. However, her recovery time was well spent. She completed work on her second book project. *Our Governors' Mansions* is a coffee table sized illustrated tour of the nation's governors' mansions. Profits from the book go to the Friends of the Mansion, Inc.

Mrs. Keating also visited 37 Oklahoma cities in 1997 and 1998, as part of the Oklahoma Department of Commerce's Main Street program, which revitalized cities and towns that had improved historic central and neighborhood business districts.

In November, 1997, the first lady hosted the first Oklahoma Summit on Children at the University of Central Oklahoma in Edmond. The purpose of the conference, attended by 300 participants, was to enlighten Oklahomans on vital issues critical to the future of children and youth.

In May, 1998, The Phillips Pavilion, a spacious covered facility, was built east of the mansion, adjacent to the swimming pool which is shaped like the state of Oklahoma. The pavilion was named for Phillips 66, the early oil company that drilled one of the first wells on grounds of the Capitol complex. The 4,700-square-foot facility was privately funded. Phillips Petroleum Company gave $300,000 of the $1.6 million

The mansion grounds were alive with children as part of the 1997 Septemberfest for children. Governor Frank Keating entertained children by telling stories in his own special camp. The event taught participants how early Oklahoma farmers harvested their crops and used Oklahoma products to create crafts. Septemberfest featured hands-on agricultural experiences such as sheep shearing, cow milking, bread making, and a petting zoo. There also was a "Trail of Tears Virtual Reality Tour." Courtesy Frank and Cathy Keating.

Below: First Lady Cathy Keating and Governor Frank Keating at the Millennium party held at the Phillips Pavilion at the mansion on December 31, 1999. Christmas lights in the trees on the mansion grounds were reflected in the Pavilion's pool and glass walls, which, coupled with the swags of tulle interlaced with lights, were truly picturesque. Guests were invited to dance their way into the new century to the music of the Mark Allen Jazz Trio from Oklahoma City University. Courtesy Fran Grounds.

cost of construction. Other donors included Conoco Inc, Oklahoma Natural Gas Company, Oklahoma Gas and Electric Services, the Helmerich Foundation, the Noble Foundation, Marie and Jimmie Austin of Seminole, John E. Kirkpatrick, LaDonna and Herman Meinders, AAON, FlintCo Inc., Frankfurt Short Bruza architects, Whirlpool Corporation, Southwestern Bell Telephone Company, Elisabeth and James Ewing, and Nedra and Robert Funt.

The Phillips Pavilion solved the long-standing problem of inadequate space in the mansion to host large receptions and dinners. Before the pavilion was built, groups of more than 60 had to be served from makeshift tents. The new pavilion accommodates 225 people for seated dinners and 500 for receptions. It is equipped with restrooms and a large kitchen. A gift shop selling Oklahoma treasures is housed in the pavilion. The proceeds benefit the Friends of the Mansion fund. An auxiliary gift shop is open on the ground floor of the State Capitol.

To remedy acoustical problems in the Phillips Pavilion, a room-sized Oriental rug was commissioned by Joe Majma and the Mathis Brothers Furniture Company of Oklahoma City. The rug is reportedly the second largest of its kind ever made in India. The rug provides warmth for meetings or events held on cold winter days in the pavilion.

Mrs. Keating hosted a Mother's Day celebration at the mansion in 1997. More than 8,000 people attended on a rainy Sunday afternoon. The purpose of the event was to recognize the importance of Oklahoma's mothers.

Also in 1997, the Keatings sponsored the first Septemberfest at the mansion. They hoped it would become a fall traditional celebration honoring Oklahoma culture and history, art, and entertainment. The governor volunteered to milk a cow. Vintage farm equipment was on display and the art of basket making and weaving was demonstrated. Oklahoma Farm Bureau held a hay maze activity for children. A petting zoo, including dairy cattle, horses, mules, baby pigs, and pygmy goats, was hosted by the Edmond Future Farmers of America chapter. Dozens of other organizations participated in the fun event.

Governor Keating was easily re-elected by Oklahoma voters in 1998, only the second governor in state history granted a second term back to back. The first lady wore a purple velvet gown with a scooped neck top and long satin skirt to the inaugural ball at the National Cowboy Hall of Fame. Oklahoma's own Shawntel Smith, Miss America 1996, sang the *National Anthem* and Dr. Robert Schuller gave the invocation as the glitter of the inaugural ball unfolded. A thousand guests crowded the National Cowboy Hall of Fame while another thousand crammed the dance floor a mile away at the Omniplex. A newspaper account said every stretch limousine in town appeared to have been in use for the event. A pre-inaugural reception and dance was held in Ponca City at the Marland Mansion.

Guests at a reception for special visitors to the inaugural ball were given porcelain boxes with star insignias and the governor's signature as mementos. The star insignia was used in the campaign for statehood and stood for Oklahoma's past. The signature of Governor Keating was a symbol of the future. He was the governor to bridge two centuries, and two millennia, for Oklahoma. He said, "In the 21st century Oklahoma will be the 'star' of the states."

The Keatings were dog lovers. While living in Washington, D.C., they named their Golden Retriever puppy "Sooner." Because Governor Keating wanted to support the University of Oklahoma and Oklahoma State University equally, the Keatings named a new black Labrador puppy "Poke," or "the Governor's Pokie Okie." Poke was hit by a car and killed in 1996. He was buried on the mansion grounds, alongside the graves of other pets lost by previous first families.

In 1999, the governor and first lady hosted a daylong conference of key policy makers and experts on marriage. *The Daily Oklahoman* applauded the Keating efforts, editorializing, "The Keatings are taking positive steps to lead what is perhaps the most difficult and necessary debate of this era: how to restore strength and stability to the sacred institution of marriage."

Above: The guardhouse at the governor's mansion was renovated in 1997. New gates allowed entrance on both sides of the facility. Traffic could be directed to the mansion or to the Phillips Pavillion. Courtesy Stuart Ostler.

The area rug in the entry hall, or foyer, is woven with the names of Oklahoma Indian tribes and tribal towns. Courtesy Michael Ives and Ackerman McQueen.

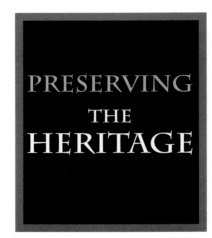

PRESERVING THE HERITAGE

THE OKLAHOMA ROOM, or living room, features a 19th century Montgolfier French hand-cut crystal chandelier, a gift of the people of Chickasha. The Chippendale Breakfront is circa 1800. On the bottom shelf are two Lenox elephants given by the Republican women of Oklahoma. All doors around the perimeter open slowly to music. Former first lady Ann Bartlett gave the Italian porcelain boxes or chests to Friends of the Mansion. The mirror in the room is original and dates from First Lady Ethel Johnston's furnishing of the mansion in 1928.

The entry hall or foyer features an ever-changing display of artwork from Oklahoma's finest galleries and museums. As a tribute to the state's rich Native American heritage, the rug has 36 federally registered Indian tribes and 3 tribal towns woven around the perimeter. Paintings were on loan from the Gilcrease Museum in Tulsa and the National Cowboy Hall of Fame and Western Heritage Center in Oklahoma City.

The runner on the stairs is a mate to the rug on the entry floor. On each riser, beginning with the second riser, are the 25 names of the governors of Oklahoma and their term of office. There are 11 empty risers, or 44 years worth of governors yet to be placed.

The 1995 renovation brought new life to the original walnut paneling in the mansion library. The Old English lectern in the corner is from the early 19th century and comes from an Old Anglican Church in England. Wing chairs are covered in Schumacher fabric. The other two chairs are in the Regency style and are covered with Brunschwig and Fils fabric. The bust of Will Rogers on the mantle was a gift from a Ponca City family. There is a working fireplace in this room.

The focal point of the hall is the replica of the silver punch bowl that was commissioned for the USS *Oklahoma*. The ebony grand piano is on loan from the Oklahoma Historical Society. The antique Baccarat crystal chandelier is new to the mansion, as is the grandfather clock. The chandelier contains stylized pineapples, the symbol for hospitality. Courtesy Stuart Ostler.

Left: The walnut paneling and molding in the library have been restored to their original beauty. The leaded glass doors cover the bookshelves that encase an impressive collection of works by Oklahoma authors. The Oklahoma Department of Libraries oversees the mansion book collection. Courtesy Michael Ives and Ackerman McQueen.

Below: The Oklahoma Room is the site of many state ceremonies. The new state seal rug, the inspiration of First Lady Cathy Keating, is already a valuable mansion heirloom. Courtesy Shane Culpepper.

Left: This stunning china, silver, and stemware were selected by First Lady Cathy Keating for use at the mansion. Patterns chosen were Royal Lapis, by Wedgwood, for formal china dinnerware; Strawberry and Vine, by Wedgwood, for casual dinnerware; China Jewel Figurine, by Lenox, for dinnerware; Richmond, by Miller and Rogaska, for stemware; and Casual, by Highlands, for casual flatware. These and many other serving pieces were donated by Oklahomans. Courtesy Michael Ives and Ackerman McQueen.

Above: The chandelier in the mansion dining room was manufactured by Smileys, Inc. of Sand Springs, Oklahoma. First Lady Shirley Bellmon purchased the chandelier to replicate one used by the Edmondsons during the 1959 renovation. First Lady Cathy Keating added the crystal ball. On the sideboard is a silver tray given in honor of Governor David Boren and a silver service donated by citizens of Billings, Oklahoma, to honor the Bellmons. At right is a French armoire. The Noble Foundation donated the Louis XV piece to the Friends of the Mansion. Courtesy Michael Ives and Ackerman McQueen.

The leaded glass doors covering the library shelves are original. Historically, they have been removed, stored, repainted, restained, and finally restored to their original location by First Lady Shirley Bellmon. In the bookshelf is a pottery vase given by former governor David Boren for Governor Frank Keating's 51st birthday. A white imperfection on the vase resembles a ghost. First Lady Cathy Keating said it must be yet another reflection of the ghost of "Alfalfa Bill" Murray.

The mansion dining room has several pieces of furniture original to the official residence. The walnut sideboard on the north wall and the dining table pedestals and all 12 chairs were purchased in 1928. The original tabletop seated only six and was changed in the 1950s and 1970s to accommodate more people.

The 12 one-of-a-kind chairs have needlepoint covers which depict the state seal; the seals of Oklahoma Indian tribes; and the state flower, mistletoe; tree, redbud; and bird, scissor tail flycatcher. The chair covers were the inspiration of First Lady Jo Hall.

The Rose Room, known as the Garden Room in previous administrations, is used as an auxiliary dining room and is adjacent to the main dining room. Original plans called the room a sunroom.

The north part of the present mansion kitchen is a fully equipped catering kitchen where food for 12 to 20 events per week is prepared. Oklahoma Natural Gas Company donated a large commercial oven. Amenities include a side-by-side refrigerator with wrap-around wine rack, 90-second dishwasher, icemaker, wine cooler, food warmer, two regular dishwashers, microwave oven, refrigerator, and a 12-burner gas cook top, donated by Oklahoma Gas and Electric Company. The cabinets in the pantry on the west wall are used for storage of food items and for serving pieces used in the dining room.

Facing page: The white wood shelving in the ballroom was redesigned in the 1995 renovation and lit to highlight gifts to the mansion. Around the room are photographs of past first families, a project completed by the Oklahoma Historical Society during the second Bellmon administration. The three chandeliers by Schonbek replaced six smaller lights, five of which were reused in other parts of the mansion. The beams are original. They were enhanced with molding and were painted white to match the rest of the ceiling. Courtesy Oklahoma Historical Society.

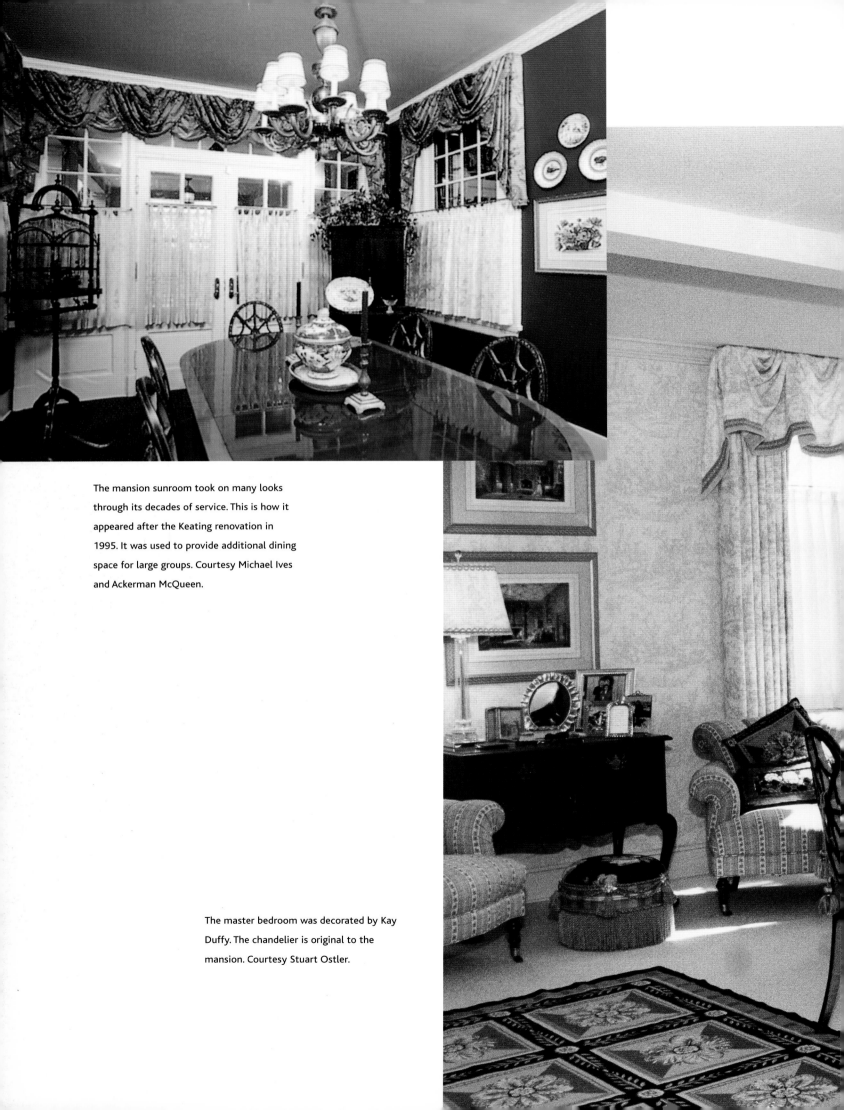

The mansion sunroom took on many looks through its decades of service. This is how it appeared after the Keating renovation in 1995. It was used to provide additional dining space for large groups. Courtesy Michael Ives and Ackerman McQueen.

The master bedroom was decorated by Kay Duffy. The chandelier is original to the mansion. Courtesy Stuart Ostler.

State dinners are prepared in the newly
renovated kitchen. State functions are
overseen by Ralph Knighton, mansion
administrator. Courtesy Michael Ives and
Ackerman McQueen.

The upstairs family room was once two rooms, the governor's bedroom and office. The furniture in the room, where most first families spend much of their time, is part of the permanent mansion collection. The grandfather clock on the west wall was purchased during the second Bellmon administration. The Italian inlaid table, which opens to a game table, is on loan from the Oklahoma Historical Society. Each first family personally owns most decorative items in the family room.

The crystal chandelier in the master bedroom on the second floor is original to the mansion. Sapulpa citizens donated the American Chippendale lowboy chest on the east wall. The painting over the bed is by Oklahoma artist Dennis Johnson. Friends of the Mansion Inc. purchased the bed. Fanny Bolen of Oklahoma City decorated both second floor bedrooms. These are used by the Keating daughters, Carrie and Kelly. Ann Henry of Oklahoma City decorated the third bedroom, occupied by college student Chip Keating on weekends and holidays.

The third floor ballroom can comfortably seat 60 people for dinner. One mile of 1920s style molding was added to the 28 x 54 room in 1995. The floors are maple and a Persian Dorokshe area rug accents the floor. The square grand Victorian-era piano dates from the Civil War and was a gift to the mansion of the Robert Hefner family.

The entire third floor was enhanced to make it more functional and inviting. There is no elevator or dumb waiter in the mansion. In the past, food was prepared and carried upstairs by hand. Dishes and

The elaborately carved Renaissance Revival mahogany bed is on loan from the Oklahoma Historical Society. It is called the Maximillian Bed because Mexican Emperor Maximillian reportedly once owned the bed. It was donated by the David Price family of Oklahoma City and is thought to have arrived in Oklahoma during the land runs. This room is where most guests stay when they visit the mansion. The first guests to stay in the room after the 1995 redecoration were Dr. and Mrs. Robert Schuller. Courtesy Michael Ives and Ackerman McQueen.

flatware also had to be carried up from the main kitchen. The 1995 renovation provided storage on the third floor for dishes, flatware, and other supplies and an auxiliary kitchen can be used to lessen the burden of carrying food from the first to the third floors for large groups of visitors.

As the new century dawned, Friends of the Mansion raised funds to acquire a unique addition to The Phillips Pavilion, a 60-by-30-foot wool rug, one of the largest hand-loomed rugs in America. Joe Majma, a rug consultant with Mathis Brothers Furniture, found a village in India where workers were willing to undertake the challenge of creating the massive rug that was installed in the Pavilion shortly before the 2000 holiday season.

First Lady Cathy Keating also oversaw an historic addition to the state china collection when she commissioned Tulsa artist Rhonda Roush in 1996 to create a new set of china and a set of hand-painted chargers. The chargers, completed in 2000, bear the seals of Oklahoma's 37 federally-recognized Indian tribes, two tribal towns, and a pair of Oklahoma state seals. Individual donors purchased place settings of the new china for the mansion in memory of family members whose names were inscribed on the plates. In the new millennium, a rich part of the state's heritage is symbolized at the mansion dinner table.

On the mansion grounds, work was underway in 2001 to renovate the old fire house for a more modern grounds management office. A grant from the Kirkpatrick Family Fund was used to rehabilitate the abandoned mansion greenhouses to produce flowers and plants for use on the mansion grounds. The greenhouses were dedicated in memory of former First Lady Shirley Bellmon.

Open house is held every Wednesday from 1:00 P.M. to 3:00 P.M. Tour guides are on hand to answer questions and pass out colorful brochures. The governor's mansion has an internet web site. The viewer can take an on-line tour of the residence and learn many interesting and historic facts.

The Oklahoma governor's mansion is endowed with a unique sense of history and state pride. The mansion's beauty is a tribute to Oklahomans, past, present, and future.

The first Oklahoma legislature envisioned a spectacular governor's mansion. However, in those early days, ample money was not available to make their dream come true. Now, in the 21st century, the residence has come full circle. A beautiful mansion, with room to entertain large groups of people in elegance and style, is a reality.

Thanks to wonderful and resilient First Ladies, the historic mansion has survived. As envisioned so long ago, Oklahoma's executive residence is one of the most beautiful homes in the state.

It is a home we can all be proud of. It is "The Home Oklahoma Built."

BIBLIOGRAPHY AND SUGGESTED READING

Apman, Patti. *Lyde Roberts Marland, The Princess of the Palace on the Prairie* (Ponca
City: Marland Mansion, 1995)

Bellmon, Henry with Pat Bellmon. *The Life and Times of Henry Bellmon* (Tulsa:
Council Oaks Books, 1992)

Blackburn, Bob L. *Heart of the Promised Land, Oklahoma County* (Woodland Hills,
California: Windsor Publications, Inc., 1982)

Bryant, Keith L., Jr. *Alfalfa Bill Murray* (Norman: University of Oklahoma Press,
1968)

Burke, Bob and Kenny L. Franks. *Dewey F. Bartlett: The Bartlett Legacy* (Edmond:
University of Central Oklahoma Press, 1996)

_____*Good Guys Wear White Hats: The Life of George Nigh* (Oklahoma City:
Oklahoma Heritage Association, 2000)

Carlile, Glenda. *Petticoats, Politics, and Pirouettes* (Oklahoma City: Southern Hills
Publishing Company, 1995)

Fischer, Leroy H. *Oklahoma's Governors, 1907-1929: Turbulent Politics* (Oklahoma City:
Oklahoma Historical Society, 1981)

_____*Oklahoma's Governors, 1929-1955 Depression to Prosperity* (Oklahoma
City: Oklahoma Historical Society, 1983)

_____*Oklahoma's Governors, 1955-1979 Growth and Reform* (Oklahoma
City: Oklahoma Historical Society, 1985)

Franks, Kenny A., Paul F. Lambert, and Carl N. Tyson. *Early Oklahoma Oil* (College
Station: Texas A & M Press, 1981)

Hines, Gordon. *Alfalfa Bill Murray An Intimate Biography* (Oklahoma City: Oklahoma
Press, 1932)

Kerr, Robert S. *Land, Wood, and Water* (New York: Fleet Publishing Corporation,
1960)

Mathews, John Joseph. *Life and Death of an Oil Man: The Career of E.W. Marland*
(Norman: University of Oklahoma Press, 1951)

Mathews, Louise. *The First Ladies of Oklahoma* (Norman: University of Oklahoma
Printing Services, 1993)

Milligan, James C. and L. David Norris. *The Man on the Second Floor: Raymond Gary*
(Muskogee: Western Heritage Books, 1988)

Morgan, Anne Hodges. *Robert S. Kerr: The Senate Years* (Norman: University Of
Oklahoma Press, 1977)

Murray, William H. *Memoirs of Governor Murray and True History of Oklahoma*
(Boston: Meador Publishing Company, 1945)

Stewart, Roy P. with Pendleton Woods. *Born Grown* (Oklahoma City: Fidelity Bank,
1974)

_____*The Turner Ranch: Master Breeder of the Hereford Line* (Oklahoma
City: Homestead Press, 1961)

Wade, Henry F. *Ship of State on a Sea of Oil* (Oklahoma City, privately printed, 1972)

Wise, Lu Celia. *Oklahoma's First Ladies* (Perkins, Oklahoma: Evans Publications, 1983)

INDEX

190